Fred DeRuvo

DECEPTION IN THE CHURCH

DOES IT MATTER HOW YOU WORSHIP?

DECEPTION IN THE CHURCH

Does It Matter How You Worship?

Fred DeRuvo

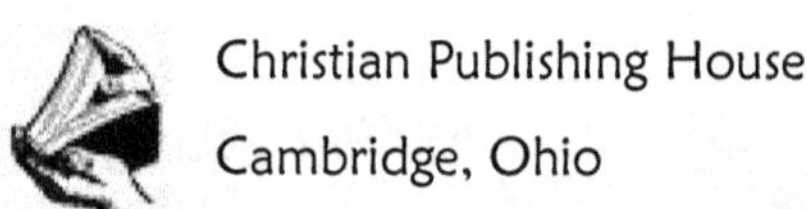
Christian Publishing House
Cambridge, Ohio

support@christianpublishers.org

DECEPTION IN THE CHURCH: Does It Matter How You Worship? by Fred DeRuvo

Editor - Whitney Rushing

ISBN-13: **978-1-945757-97-6**

ISBN-10: **1-945757-97-3**

Table of Contents

Foreword

I have noticed in these days a strange sound coming from the walls of the city. The watchmen are not crying out alarms – they are laughing. Does this mean all is well? Not by a long shot.

The Devil is a master of delusion and thus every age needs watchmen. Every watchman needs two perspectives: first, to cry out against dangerous trends emerging inside the city walls, and then, to warn against dangers lurking outside the walls. Both threats are destructive and demand constant vigilance. When the watchman discovers a real concern, he has but one duty: he must say something!

Dr. Fred DeRuvo is such a watchman and this book is such a cry.

This is a sad day. The church has traded her watchmen for clowns and charlatans. The sharp sword of truthful confrontation has been traded for the cotton candy of a smooth preachers and sloppy teachers. The King of Truth has been dethroned and the dwellers of this New Order have installed the Three Stooges of the end times called, "Oneness, Warmness, and Wonders." *Oneness* is the ruler whose mantra is unity without biblical discernment, *Warmness* cries out for a feeling of closeness to God without sound practice and *Wonders* is the ruler who attracts crowds by all things that amaze and amuse.

Perhaps you've noticed that church websites today are full of trendy buzz words about family, community, fun, and excitement. However, what is strangely lacking in our day is some good, old-fashioned Puritan "toe stomping." Sin reigns in our churches and little is said. Discernment is at half-mast. Few churches have courses on how to call out the false prophets of the day, "Ye serpents, ye generation of vipers!" *(Matthew 23:33).* Now the snakes slither freely about the sanctuary. Our watchmen are going to seed on "sensitivity training," admitting all comers to the church regardless of genuine faith or genuine doctrine. Churches are now the laughing, back-slapping, high-fiving, jiving, swaying, dancing, barking, and convulsing centers of "worship." (May that pastor beware who dares to call the church what God calls it – "the called-out ones.") Like Lot's wife, we are trying unsuccessfully to make our escape from the very culture we admire.

And what of the Word of God?

Churches are no longer measured by the Scriptures but are solely judged on the emotional impact and the warm sense of community they infuse. "If it feels right, positive, and powerful, then it must be the church for me." The leaders of these churches are not duly tested. Truly, the New Apostolic Reformers (a term used loosely for those that "bedazzle" the church) are, indeed, full of artificial hype. The movement lacks the true power of God and holy results. These new "apostles" come creeping in "with all power, and signs, and lying wonders," and I believe, are setting the table for the end times *(II Thessalonians 2:9).* Careless sheep follow unsuspectingly.

Dr. Fred DeRuvo has given us a treasure in his latest book, *Deception in the Church.* It is my privilege to endorse not only this clear expose of the "New Apostles" of our day, but to claim friendship with the author of it. God requires only two things of men who are called to leadership within the church. First, that they be men of sound doctrine, and second, that they be men of sound practice *(Titus 1:5-16).* On these two grounds alone, the author's words carry great weight with me. I know him to be, by word and life, a man of God. The fact that Dr. Fred DeRuvo speaks out about dangerous religious trends is very personal. Early on in his own journey to discover the truth, his path allowed him a first-hand experience with those who "peddle" mysterious revelations and ploy their curious craft upon many who truly want to know God. Glad now to be free of such teaching, he knows of what he speaks and warns others lovingly.

You will find this book to be a helpful apologetic for biblical truth and the true worship of God. The author's final conclusion about how to know the will of God is worth the read. His warning about the dark side of those who profess to know God yet in practice deny Him will serve as a clear warning to keep your eyes fixed on Jesus.

Our thanks to you, Fred.

Anchors upward,

Pastor Loren Regier

Introduction

I was raised in a home where my mother brought us to a Protestant church every Sunday. There were many times I did not want to go, but once I got there, it was enjoyable. My father, an ex-Catholic, was not inclined to attend church, so he rarely went with us.

As I grew older, I began to understand that there was something very important I needed to grasp for my life. I knew there was a heaven and a hell,[1] and I knew that I did not want to go to hell. I began to learn that I had a choice.

It was not until the age of thirteen, while sitting in the pew of the church we were attending that I finally realized my need and understood that Jesus had paid the price. My faith (belief) in His life and death on the cross in my place gave me the needed salvation. I recall walking down front during the altar call that morning and hearing the explanation of the gospel. Several men prayed with me as well.

I was a Christian, and my life changed! I knew it had changed because my outlook was different. I started telling my friends about Jesus and about the gospel. Many rebuffed me, and a few threatened me, but I kept it up.

Eventually, my ardor cooled a bit in what I thought at the time was a spurt of Christian maturity. I realize now of course that it was simply relaxing my relationship with God in Christ. I had not been discipled by anyone, so I was not aware of *how* to grow in Christ. In fact, I had never considered that there was more I had to do in order to grow in Christ. There were things that God expected of me, but no one told me about them. Since I was not daily reading His Word, I had no knowledge of the truth either.

Time passed, and I went to and graduated from what used to be Philadelphia College of Bible. I was "prepared" to go into ministry and I

---

[1] While **Christian Publishing House (CPH)** is publishing Deception In the Church, they would disagree with the author on the hellfire doctrine. CPH's position is that the hellfire doctrine of eternal torment is unbiblical. Below are some CPH Blog articles for the reader, so he or she can have both sides and decide for themselves.

Hellfire – Eternal Torment? (http://tiny.cc/pmnwsy) What Did Jesus Teach About Hell? (http://tiny.cc/7hnwsy) Is Hellfire Part of Divine Justice? (http://tiny.cc/gnnwsy) Is the Hellfire Doctrine Truly Just? (http://tiny.cc/0nnwsy) The Bible's Viewpoint of Death (http://tiny.cc/9nnwsy)

tried, but things did not work out. Over the next few decades I tried several times again to move into ministry, but things never seemed to work out.

Because I knew I was not living the life God wanted me to live, I eventually became attracted to the Charismatic Movement in the 1970s as it offered "something more." What I thought was going to open the door to a deeper, more spiritual life for me did the exact opposite. I'll discuss more of that in this book.

I also failed to understand the actual origins of the Charismatic Movement, as it was an outgrowth of New Order of Latter Rain (NOLR). I failed to grasp that the underlying motive of the Charismatic Movement was a great push toward unity through *ecumenism.* I will also discuss this in these pages.

The Charismatic Movement, like movements before it, including NOLR, focused people on their subjective feelings to determine God's will. Christendom needed to do away with the dead formality and traditionalism that had enveloped mainline denominations and instead, learn to sense the Spirit's moving through subjectivity. God's Word was still used, but only to buttress the "new" revelations and prophecies put forth by leaders within the Charismatic Movement.

For the Charismatic, emotions are the barometer of discernment in living the Christian life. This was not only part of the Charismatic Movement in the 1970s but is clearly seen in the way many leaders within evangelical Christianity broadcast their messages to us today.

In modern America at the turn of the 1900s, the Asuza Street Revival of 1906 marks the beginning of the movements that have morphed into what is now known as the New Apostolic Reformation (or NAR). We will highlight the many shades of this movement through the decades that have brought us to where we are now. For the lack of a better label, we might call all of these various movements and offshoots, "the Signs and Wonders Movements." We do so because that undergirds each segment of the various movements through the decades to the present.

We will also spend some time dissecting many of the specific teachings of those within the Signs and Wonders Movements, comparing those teachings to the Bible. Are they in agreement with God's Word or do they go off on their own path? Because of my own personal past involvement in the Charismatic Movement, my firsthand experience will be noted when relevant. Beyond this, we will compare many of the same teachings to those taught within the New Age. Will we find differences or commonalities?

Characteristically, the Signs and Wonders Movements always focus on a new "work" God is doing. That "new" thing is always in the form of some sort of revival. There, the emphasis is on not only what God is doing, but on the Christian's responsibility (allegedly) to be open to God's new work. When God manifests Himself in a variety of supernatural and ecstatic ways, we are told that we should not squelch the Spirit. We should embrace whatever new thing God is doing. To squelch it creates the dead formalism found in traditional mainline denomination churches.

In this book, I will discuss any problems that may come to the fore with this type of thinking and teaching. Ultimately, we will see whether ecstatic experiences are the things God uses to mature His children and direct their steps.

I will also present what I believe is the biblical approach to living out God's will for our lives and how to determine whether any so-called "new works" of God are actually *from* God in the first place. Thank you for joining me on this journey.

CHAPTER 1 Something Insidious This Way Grows

The basic definition of a cult is a group of people whose beliefs are opposed to one or more of the orthodox or fundamental beliefs long held within Christianity. Many cults have been catalogued over the years by numerous authors like Walter Martin (*Kingdom of the Cults*).

One of the more basic cultic beliefs is the denial of the full deity of Jesus. Other cults might deny the all-sufficiency of Scripture. Still, others insist that salvation comes not through faith alone, by grace alone, in Christ alone, but by *earning* it either to receive it initially or to maintain it. Without constant maintenance, it is alleged that salvation can be lost. In short, cults normally go *beyond* the confines of Scripture by either adding to it or misconstruing it for their own purposes. Error is the result in both cases.

Cults are a plague within Christendom because of their ability to lead people astray. Cult leaders often use Christian-sounding verbiage that causes people to lower their defenses as they think they are orthodox in their beliefs. However, a closer look at their beliefs proves they are not.

One religious cult, in particular, has been around for decades, and its leaders and proponents are often heard bragging about its exponential growth. The movement itself indirectly dates back to the 1906 Azusa Street Revival of Los Angeles, though it got its big start in Canada in 1948. With nearly every successive decade since that time, the name and leadership has changed. Regardless of this, the emphasis of the movement has always remained the same though its name has changed several times.

This particular cult has actually become epidemic in scale because of its ability to infiltrate known and established portions of evangelicalism. Today, well-known Christian leaders appear to be moving away from the truth they once claimed and are now embracing ideas and concepts promulgated by this cult, which has more in common with the New Age Movement (secular humanism), than with orthodox Christianity.

Australia's lead pastor of Hillsong Church appeared on *The View* in 2017 with biblically compromising opinions on abortion and homosexuality. Another well-known author and speaker appear to be sanctioning what he calls "Christian hedonism." Still, others have committed themselves to or embraced aspects of Roman Catholicism or the Greek Orthodox faith. What is going on here?

The sad truth seems to be that leaders we once thought faithful to orthodoxy are now, in many ways, simply abandoning the faith in favor of something else altogether. It is very clear that these leaders (and many others too numerous to list here) appear to have something in common. They have jettisoned God's Word in favor of determining truth through their *subjectivity.*

"Truth" through subjectivity is a major characteristic of how the world thinks as seen in the many forms of *political correctness* that permeate society today. Subjectivity, specifically, is also very much part of New Age thought and comprises a huge core within NAR.

Within the secular New Age arena, each person determines his own truth for himself, and that truth may be different for someone else. Subjective truth, of course, is not truth at all, but simply *opinion* masquerading as truth. Not surprisingly, New Age truth or "political correctness" appears to be similar from one person to the next but often equally opposed to biblical truth.

Certain leaders within Christendom now teach that there exists more than one path to God, or that Jesus is divine but not *the* God. They also teach that God wants us to have fun and enjoy life. Many also teach that it is detrimental to discuss sin and its deadly consequences for fear of pushing people away from Jesus.

All of these aberrant teachings stem from the same lie. That lie is at the very heart of the New Age Movement and at its core, secular humanism. That same lie has also been a part of the newest cult that has captured the hearts and minds of thousands in the evangelical church throughout the world. This lie is that truth is a movable palette determined by how we *feel* about things, not based on the absolute truth of Scripture.

The cult that has risen to the top over the past number of decades is now called the *New Apostolic Reformation,* or NAR, for short. Like the New Age and secular humanism, it has been making serious in-roads into evangelicalism. It stands against Christian orthodoxy. It has also ultimately been pulling people *out of* evangelical circles into its own fold. This is truly unfortunate, leading one to wonder if NAR is part of the "delusion" Paul mentions that creates such apostasy in the end times (II Thessalonians 2:11; II Timothy 3:1-5).

Note Peter's words regarding how these false teachers would infiltrate and affect the church.

But false prophets also arose among the people, just as there will be false teachers among you, who will secretly bring in destructive heresies, even denying the Master who bought them, bringing upon themselves swift destruction. And many will follow their sensuality, and because of them the way of truth will be blasphemed. And ***in their greed they will exploit you with false words****. Their condemnation from long ago is not idle, and their destruction is not asleep. (II Peter 2:1-3, emphasis added)*

The tragedy is that many who began the race well appear to have gotten seriously off the path. These individuals seem to be enamored with *ecumenism*, a desire for unity despite differences in theological beliefs. They agree with the call for a cessation of teaching those "troublesome" doctrines and Bible truths that simply make people feel guilty (sin, hell, eternal death, etc.). "Away with that," they say!

In the above Scripture, the apostle Peter tells his readers that false prophets arose among the people in times past, referring to *Israel.* He is stating that truth was diluted because people already living among the Israelites and possibly in leadership positions came out with false teachings and false prophecies. Peter implies they did what they did for financial gain ("*...their greed will exploit you...*"). The same then applies to the false prophets and teachers of today. Peter would argue that they also do what they do to exploit Christians and for their own financial gain.

We see this theme repeatedly throughout the Old Testament prophets. These false teachers and prophets often stood against true prophets of God whom He had raised up to deliver His message to Israel. Balaam is just one false prophet who did what he did for self-aggrandizement and financial gain *(Numbers 22:1-35; Matthew 24:14).*

This situation existed during Jesus' day as well, as He often went head-to-head with the religious leaders of His day, the Scribes, the Pharisees, and the Sadducees. In essence, those individuals, due to their deluded state, which stemmed from their rebellious and hardened hearts, withstood Jesus every chance they had due to their jealousy. They did so to protect their own lifestyles and positions they held in the community. This very thing is happening today.

Rev. James Stalker notes that these Old Testament false prophets "*culminated in the lifetime of Jeremiah, whose whole career might almost be described as a conflict with them. Again and again he and they came to open war; and on at least one occasion the whole body combined to take away his life. Ezekiel was scarcely less afflicted by them. They were perhaps not so prominent an element in the life of Isaiah, but he also refers to them frequently; and, indeed, their sinister figures haunt the pages of all the prophets.*"[2]

God Himself responded to these false prophets through the mouths of the prophets, telling them in no uncertain terms there would come a day when false prophecies would no longer be heard and no "divination" would be part of Israel *(Ezekiel 12:24).* We are not there yet. We are, however, on the cusp of something huge as God's Word continues to unfold and these false prophets of today come to the fore.

In fact, the situation with Elijah, Mt. Carmel, and the prophets of Baal proves that at times, God chose not to wait until His physical return to deal with these false prophets. Often, He chose to deal with them directly and eradicate them from the face of the earth *(I Kings 18).* Note that in that situation, Elijah killed the 450 prophets of Baal who withstood him and God *(v. 40).*

In Peter's case, he acknowledged that in Old Testament times false prophets existed who actually rose up among (or from) the people of Israel. Peter stated that the very same thing would happen within the Christian community.

Peter says, "*...just as there will be false teachers among you.*" The apostle warned the flock that this would occur. He did not say it was a possibility. He said it *would* happen.

Peter even tells his readers (including us) *how* this will occur. The false teachers would *secretly* bring in destructive heresies. This is exactly what cults do by teaching untruths with Christian sounding terms. These heresies create division in the flock through confusion. It is often difficult for the average Christian to know and understand the truth, especially for those who rarely read or study God's Word.

The apostle John is even more specific concerning heretical viewpoints as the end of this age approaches.

Children, it is the last hour, and as you have heard that antichrist is coming, so now many antichrists have come. Therefore we know that it is the last hour. They went out from us, but they were not of us; for if they had been of us, they would have continued with us. But they went out, that it might become plain that they all are not of us. (I John 2:18-19)

Note that John says that certain individuals "*went out from us, but they were not of us.*" Clearly, they only *appeared* to be part of the true

[2] http://watch-unto-prayer.org/stalker.html (12/20/2017)

flock because they were part of it *physically*. However, they eventually "came out" to be seen for what they were – false teachers whose mission it was to attempt to destroy God's truth, capturing the flock with their lies.

A successful con artist gains mastery over victims by mixing truth with lies. At least in the beginning, the lies are often very small, barely perceptible, but over time, they become broader in scope. Too often by then, it is too late to notice because people have already succumbed to those lies. The lies are not recognized because they have become so ingrained within them. They actually become angry with someone trying to point out the lies they now believe as truth. They see that person as narrow-minded, bigoted, or worse, an enemy of God.

Many Christian leaders today water down the gospel, with a growing number saying that people do not have to be Christians to have a relationship with God. This is becoming very prevalent within many so-called "evangelical churches." In reality, these churches align themselves more with the error that exists in the New Age movement and in the New Apostolic Reformation (NAR). The entire push has been a form of ecumenism.

Because of the division and tension that results from this errant teaching, these so-called Christian leaders step forward "begging" for *unity* among Christians. They take Christians to task and attempt to shame them for not going along with the program.

They argue that this disagreement over "words" (it is actually *doctrine* that is of concern here) should not exist because it sends the wrong message to the world. The world sees Christians in disunity, and the lost are pushed away from God because of it. To correct this, leaders urge Christians to set aside theological differences and come together for the "cause" of Christ. The world then will see our "love" (contrived unity and come to Jesus. This is *not* the model set for us in the Bible. However, it has been at the heart of the various movements that have occurred across the decades. I will discuss this more in-depth later.

In the scenario described above (where unity reigns after ignoring all theological differences), *if* the lost turn to Jesus, to which Jesus will they be turning? If there is a compromise of doctrinal truth about who He is, what He accomplished for us, and His plans and purposes for humanity and the earth, then the "Jesus" the lost will turn to is nothing more than the "New Age Jesus," who in reality is ultimately the Antichrist. That particular "Jesus" (Antichrist) offers nothing because that "Jesus" is not God Almighty. He will merely be *a god*; a man who is satanically inspired and indwelt.

The New Age teaches that this is what all human beings are capable of becoming as well (little gods), since we all have the divine spark within us.

This belief is understood as the "Christ Consciousness." It is also the spirit of the Antichrist because it denies the truth about our Lord and Savior *(I John 2:2)*. Is this where NAR is ultimately leading us to? Does NAR offer any teachings that align more with the New Age movement than with the Bible? I will seek to answer that question in this book.

Attorney Constance Cumbey has been writing about this slide into the New Age Movement by the visible church for decades. Her first book, *The Hidden Dangers of the Rainbow* (1983), was followed by *A Planned Deception: The Staging of the New Age Messiah* (1985). These two books show how Cumbey believes Satan has been working to incorporate the visible church into the realm of the New Age Movement, effectively blinding people to the truth about God in Christ.

*Today, the New Age Movement and other components of the New World Order have infiltrated the Bible-believing churches and Christian ministries. According to Constance Cumbey, their expressed goal is to **use the evangelical church** as the primary instrument to bring the New World Order to birth.[3] (emphasis added)*

Cumbey outlines this in the two books just mentioned. It is simply too much of a coincidence to hear so many leaders within NAR using terms and verbiage that is common within the New Age Movement.

Beware of false prophets, who come to you in sheep's clothing but inwardly are ravenous wolves. You will recognize them by their fruits. Are grapes gathered from thornbushes, or figs from thistles? So, every healthy tree bears good fruit, but the diseased tree bears bad fruit. A healthy tree cannot bear bad fruit, nor can a diseased tree bear good fruit. Every tree that does not bear good fruit is cut down and thrown into the fire. Thus you will recognize them by their fruits. (Matthew 7:15-20)

So why do so many seemingly sincere Christians seem to fall for the bells, baubles, and false teachings of what clearly resembles the New Age Movement, though its name is New Apostolic Reformation?

---

[3] http://watch-unto-prayer.org/watch.html (12/20/2017)

CHAPTER 2 Growing Ecumenical Deception: Apostasy

The Bible foretells of a time that is coming when people will no longer care to listen to sound doctrine. They will prefer to hear what makes them *feel good.* In short, *experience* will be their preferred teacher, not God's Word. That time seems to be clearly upon us.

For the time is coming when people will not endure sound teaching, but having itching ears they will accumulate for themselves teachers to suit their own passions... (II Timothy 4:3)

I was involved in the Charismatic Movement in the mid-1970s and remained there for several years. When I ultimately left Charismania, it was because I had gotten to the point of not being able to line up many teachings and experiences there with Scripture. In fact, I learned that much within the movement opposed biblical truth.

Prophetic words of knowledge and tongues are forms of ecstatic experiences. These are prevalent and were routinely accepted as manifestations of God's presence during my time in the Charismatic Movement. It is still the same today with New Apostolic Reformation (NAR), which grew out of the Charismatic Movement decades before.

Aside from signs and wonders and ecstatic experiences, the one other main doctrine that is pushed is a form of ecumenism. This is huge, and I will deal with this in detail later. But it is good for readers to know and understand that regardless of what the particular movement of a specific decade was called, the emphasis of that movement *always* included an ecumenical spirit.

This unbiblical concept – moving the church toward ecumenism - has been heralded among the signs and wonders people, with the twisting of Scripture to "prove" that this is what God wants. However, it is clear enough from Scripture that this is *not* what God wants, but what He will *allow* to occur in order that Satan will be able to introduce his man – the final man of sin *(II Thessalonians 2)*, or the Antichrist, as ruler of the final human kingdom (Revised Roman Empire) at the end of this age. The Antichrist will be destroyed by Jesus at His second coming.

That the world will become "one" in unified purposes is *not* a good thing, except for the fact that Jesus will ultimately return and destroy the Antichrist. However, for the world to get to that future point of a false secular religious unity (not unlike the attempted unity at the Tower of

Babel; Genesis 11), the spirit of the Antichrist must be allowed and encouraged to permeate society globally.

The Bible teaches that apostasy within Christendom will become a major global problem that will feed into the things that Satan is attempting to accomplish. This is very clear from passages of Scripture from Jesus (Olivet Discourse, Matthew 24, Mark 13, Luke 21), and Paul, Peter, and other writers as well.

This growing evil and the apostasy that will result from it will work hand in hand to bring Satan's final kingdom to the fore, headed up by the Antichrist. Regarding the current, growing apostasy the Bible warns about, the one main reason for its occurrence is clearly spelled out in Scripture. No guesswork is needed on our part.

God clearly describes why these things are going to occur to an ever-increasing degree as the time of His second coming approaches. Let us start with Paul's words from II Thessalonians 2:7-12.

For the mystery of lawlessness is already at work. Only he who now restrains it will do so until he is out of the way. And then the lawless one will be revealed, whom the Lord Jesus will kill with the breath of his mouth and bring to nothing by the appearance of his coming. The coming of the lawless one is by the activity of Satan with all power and false signs and wonders, and with all wicked deception for those who are perishing...

I deliberately stopped in the middle of verse 10, but we will finish this section in a moment. Notice that even during Paul's day, he warned his readers that the "*mystery of lawlessness*" already existed and was working its way throughout society just as yeast works its way throughout an entire loaf of bread.

Exactly what is this "*mystery of lawlessness*" Paul speaks of here? In a general sense, this "mystery" (truth not previously revealed) of "lawlessness" refers to the growing sense of contempt for law and order. We are certainly seeing that on a large-scale. While the FBI says some crime is down over the past few years, violent crime and lawlessness, in general, has increased.[4] In fact, look at the amount of so-called "sanctuary cities" in America. This is very loosely based on the Old Testament cities of refuge where a person who had *accidentally* killed another could go for refuge *(Exodus 21:13)*.

The concept of an American sanctuary city overthrows the biblical idea. Today, people who are illegally in the United States and commit

[4] https://www.fbi.gov/news/stories/latest-crime-statistics-released (06/29/2018)

crimes are often protected from arrest or prosecution in these cities. We witnessed this recently in the Kate Steinle case in San Francisco, CA, in which an illegal immigrant had an illegal weapon and killed Kate in front of her family. He was arrested and put on trial and was found not guilty of all charges. This is reprehensible as it turns justice on its head.[5] However, it is clear that this type of mentality is becoming more prominent in America and the world. It is pure lawlessness.

Lawless people have always been a part of society, with some centuries evidencing more lawlessness than others. However, Paul is saying that at some specific point in the future, this lawlessness will increase greatly. Paul is speaking about "*the revelation of a future climax of lawlessness that would follow the removal of the restrainer*"[6] that he just referred to in verse seven.

Paul is saying that God is keeping the full measure of lawlessness, or anarchy, at bay until the appointed time when the restrainer is removed or taken out of the way. Once that restraining influence is gone, society will become exponentially more lawless as it prepares to make way for the coming Antichrist.

However, *why* does this occur? The answer is in the second portion of II Thessalonians 2:10.

10(b)...because they refused to love the truth and so be saved. 11 Therefore God sends them a strong delusion, so that they may believe what is false, 12 in order that all may be condemned who did not believe the truth but had pleasure in unrighteousness. (emphasis added)

The reason lawlessness will increase will be due to man's refusal to love the truth and be saved. In other words, the truth Paul refers to is *the* truth about Jesus Christ and salvation. That truth is the only truth that can save people. However, there will be a growing rejection of such truth. It is happening now.

This same idea is echoed in the Old Testament in places like Psalm 2. Humanity in general, like Satan, does not want God to be ruler over the earth. Satan's attitude is clearly reflected in and throughout much of society.

Nevertheless, what does this have to do with the church or at least, with Christendom? The Bible tells us that Christians must give up serving *self*. We are to instead, adopt God's perspective *daily* since we are new

---

[5] https://legalinsurrection.com/2017/11/kate-steinles-accused-killer-acquitted/ (06/29/2018)

[6] Dr. Constable's Notes on Thessalonians, p. 19

creations *(II Corinthians 5:17).* We are to put Him and His will *first.* Once we receive salvation, we are to spend our remaining days living for God.

Becoming saved means the Holy Spirit indwells and seals us unto the day of redemption *(Ephesians 1:13).* His indwelling presence makes it possible to truly serve Him and His purposes from our hearts, not simply with outward actions. Serving Him daily must be a conscious, continual decision on our part, often moment by moment. Of course, Satan is always on hand to make that very difficult.

The sincere, devout Christian often wants "more" of God. We reason because God is ethereal, supernatural, and all-powerful, it is naturally assumed that our relationship with Him should *also* be ethereal, supernatural, and powerful (to a degree).

Some teach that if this is not the norm for Christians, those Christians are doing something wrong and it must be corrected. In order to correct it, Christians must learn to expect and rely on *experience* with God, not necessarily knowledge based in His Word of Truth, the Bible.

The teachers who emphasize this line of thinking will say that experience with God reveals more of Him. Therefore, we should not eschew the experiences. They will give lip service to the idea that the spirits should be tested *(I John 4:1),* but rarely did I ever hear anyone warn of the possibility of being deceived or deluded during my time spent in the Charismatic Movement.

In fact, I cannot recall one instance of any leader warning anyone during all the meetings I attended of potential fraud from demonic spirits masquerading as angels of light *(II Corinthians 11:14).* The same can be said of today's meetings, books, and video conferences within NAR. There is only constant encouragement to open one's self to the Spirit of God and allow Him to work, however, that "work" may appear and whatever the true source of that work happens to be.

There are a plethora of videos on the internet where viewers will see people fully anticipating what is about to happen. They appear to long for it, wait for it, and want it badly. There is no warning at all from leaders even when demonic manifestations appear to break out. People simply smile benignly as they help people to the floor and let what happens, happen.

It is very disconcerting to see what is happening today. It is the result of the continuing push of the Charismatic Movement and its various offshoots like NAR into society, often with leaders stating that God is doing "something new." Normally, this "something new" is in new experiences.

Conferences are held across America touting unity within Christendom. Still I have yet to see any serious, lasting change in people as a result of these gatherings, except the watering down of sound doctrine. That is the only real change.

Solid doctrine is being pushed out the door for the sake of unity, which then translates to "brotherly love," and all is based on ecstatic experiences, which have no lasting value and do not mature the Christian in his faith. Where is the Fruit of the Spirit? That would be true evidence of God's hand in these situations.

But the fruit of the Spirit is love, joy, peace, patience, kindness, goodness, faithfulness, gentleness, self-control; against such things there is no law. (Galatians 5:22-23)

Unfortunately, self-control is not only the last thing that is evidenced at many of these conferences, events, and gatherings. It is often completely absent. That alone should make people question the validity of the experiences they seek and whether they are from God, Satan, or self.

As stated, the growing thought within Christendom is that we must practice and embrace "unity" regardless of the many conflicting and even egregious teachings regarding God as compared to His Word. This push toward unity ultimately means never disagreeing with anyone who does not share your views. If we disagree, the world will see and label Christians as hypocrites.

Yet Jesus, Paul, and others routinely disagreed with religious leaders who did not teach truth, and they did so out of love for them and love for truth itself. Jesus called Himself "Truth" in John 14:6.

Jesus said to him, "I am the way, and the truth, and the life. No one comes to the Father except through me.

Today, it is not politically correct to teach someone what the Bible actually says and that it only has one meaning. That is seen as bigoted, judgmental, egotistical, or even as the late Tony Palmer has intimated, "spiritual racism." I will talk more about that later.

CHAPTER 3 Growing Ecumenical Deception: Contrived Unity

In our last chapter, we introduced the subject of the growing ecumenical deception that is taking hold of large areas of Christendom. We noted that this push toward unity (ecumenism) had been part of each decade since 1948 when New Order of Latter Rain (NOLR) began in Canada. This has also been evidenced within the Charismatic Movement (CM). It was also part of the Shepherding and the Purpose Driven Movements which came after it. It is now being pushed by NAR and endorsed by the Roman Catholic Church (RCC).

It is important to understand that ecumenism has undergirded each of these movements alleged to have been from God. The call to set aside theological differences drove the Shepherding and Purpose Driven Movements. Christians were told to do so out of love for others. Setting aside doctrinal differences and simply embracing people in spite of any differences was the very definition of love, we were told. It is the same today with the New Apostolic Reformation (NAR).

It is alleged that God is moving. He is no respecter of persons. He doesn't care about a person's background. He simply wants people to come to Him. While God certainly does want people to come to Him, He wants them to come in *repentance* and *humility*. He wants people to understand that they are sinners and that sin keeps them away from a holy God. However, He made it possible for us to return to Him through the life, death, and resurrection of Jesus. Because of that, He has the right to demand that people approach Him in the way He desires.

However, the exact opposite appears to be on display throughout NAR. In what is known as "Sloshfests," being drunk in the Spirit, slain in the Spirit, babbling incoherently, cackling laughter and animal sounds from people who attend many NAR events are the norm. All this is supposed evidence of God moving among people.

I will unpack this more in detail, but sufficed to say that *if* the things experienced and witnessed during these NAR meetings (or like the Charismatic meetings I attended years ago) are supposed to be of God, then why is there so much instruction about what it means to be a mature Christian? Why does the Bible spend time explaining to us how the character of Jesus should look in each Christian?

Because people today have become so dependent on (and actually go out of their way to seek), new "words" and "revelations" from God, all manner of aberrant theology is the result. This in turn often shipwrecks people's faith. It does so because of the use of ***subjectivity*** to determine truth. God does not want nor expects us to use our feelings to determine the truthfulness of any situation. He has provided His all-sufficient Word for that. However, if we never read it, study it, or memorize it, we will not be able to use it as the powerful weapon it is against all heresy and doctrines of demons.

I do not intend to judge people's motives or the condition of their hearts as I provide examples throughout this book, whether they are lay people or leaders within NAR. I am doing our best to assess what leaders in that movement *teach*. That is my concern.

For too many today, the idea of theological differences is anathema. We are told we should avoid it at all costs to keep from offending people and pushing them away from the gospel of Jesus. Of course, Paul addressed this in his epistle to the Corinthian believers when he stated the following:

For the word of the cross is folly to those who are perishing, but to us who are being saved it is the power of God. (I Corinthians 1:18)

Only those people whose eyes are opened by the living God will not see the gospel message (word of the cross) as foolishness. They will come to see it as the salvation it represents.

However, it is fast becoming politically *incorrect* to preach the gospel itself or to voice concerns over theological error. We should not claim that the Bible is the absolute truth. We should at most state that it is truth *for us*, but to say more is to offend others.

Jesus, Paul, Peter, and others in the New Testament had no such concerns. They normally met error head-on. As Christians, we are to do the same, *in love*, yes, but we must do what they did. Before we can do that, however, we must learn and know what God's Word actually says.

Because of this push toward contrived unity (ecumenism) through the de-emphasis of doctrine and theology, it appears that Christianity is being hijacked, morphed into something else entirely. Those who refuse to embrace this new version of "Christianity" are divisive, judgmental, spiritual racists, legalistic, Pharisaic, and worse.

For the remainder of this chapter, we will focus on some of the teachings and experiences that are part of the Charismatic Movement, which has become what today is known as the world's newest cult; the New Apostolic Reformation (NAR). For brevity's sake, I will refer to New Apostolic Reformation as simply NAR from here on out.

There are many articles and videos on the internet about NAR. *Church Watch Central* has a storehouse of up-to-date articles highlighting the movement from its origins to the present, with its many inceptions and names. One article, in particular, includes many audio links that flesh out the truth about NAR[7] often from NAR leaders themselves.

There are many theological problems with NAR's belief system. They essentially have a different gospel yet use verbiage that we are all familiar with so as not to raise any red flags. This is often done deliberately, as evidenced by use of the same by the many cults before NAR (Jehovah's Witnesses, Mormonism, Christian Science, etc.). These older cults also use many Christian-sounding terms but of course, apply their own unique meaning. Most people upon hearing familiar terms, generally accept what is said as biblical and apply their own traditional or orthodox meaning to the terms they hear. It is in this way that cults like NAR flourish.

With respect to salvation or the gospel itself, the emphasis within NAR is not about introducing people to authentic *salvation* available only in Jesus. In fact, watching many of the videos of NAR events bears this out.

During NAR gatherings, the authentic gospel of Jesus is never presented. There is a good deal of upbeat music, praying, and an overabundance of *prophesying* about what God is allegedly going to do in the world. Then the many ecstatic experiences purported to be manifestations of God's presence begin to occur throughout the arena.

I have yet to witness a clear presentation of the gospel at these events. There is never an altar call where people are invited forward for the purpose of explaining *salvation* to them one-on-one, nor is there prayer specifically for salvation. There *are* altar calls of a sort, but normally for the purpose of receiving whatever God is apparently dolling out. Because things are so earnestly nebulous at these events, one can only wonder just exactly what is being taught, much less, what people are actually receiving. As it is, it is not the gospel as presented in Scripture.

For NAR, the biblical gospel is downplayed while their version of the gospel is exalted. "*The NAR Gospel: The Gospel of the Kingdom is all about bringing heaven to earth and manifesting the presence of God on the earth which MUST happen in all fullness in order to trigger Christ's return.*"[8] It is all about Christians working to bring God's Kingdom to earth, as though God cannot do this without Christians helping to make it happen. Christians

---

7 https://churchwatchcentral.com/2017/05/06/resource-what-is-the-nar/ (12/20/2017)

8 https://churchwatchcentral.com/2017/05/06/resource-what-is-the-nar/ (12/20/2017)

can only do this, we are told, through an ecumenical spirit. That is how God works, according to NAR.

Of course, this is not the biblical concept at all. Jesus commissioned His apostles and disciples to, "*Go therefore and make disciples of all nations, baptizing them in the name of the Father and of the Son and of the Holy Spirit, teaching them to observe all that I have commanded you. And behold, I am with you always, to the end of the age.*" *(Matthew 28:19-20)*

There is nothing to indicate that Christians are to wrest control of this earth from Satan and his minions so that Jesus will finally be in a position to be *able* to return to earth. The very idea is filled with hubris and denies God's sovereignty. Jesus' reference to "nations" in the above text is really speaking about individual people *from* all the various nations, not the nations or governing bodies of those nations.

Along these lines, there is the belief that a massive, end times revival will occur once Christians get it together, set aside differences, and join in unity of purpose. "*NAR Apostle Lance Wallnau preaches the Gospel of the Kingdom and exalts it above Christ's gospel of salvation and his belief that the Gospel of the Kingdom is being restored to the church in all its power to bring an end-times army/revival.*"[9]

This really all harkens back to a man named David J. DuPlessis, also known as "Mr. Pentecost." His name was huge during the time I was involved in the Charismatic Movement. He was seen as almost a demi-god. People wanted to get close to him. They wanted to absorb the spirit that motivated him.

While I never met DuPlessis, I was familiar with his teachings. Because of my lack of biblical knowledge at the time, he seemed right on to me. Now, looking back and reading some of his articles and sermons, all I can think is "What demon was operating through him to print such religious gobbledygook?" I mean no disrespect, but too many of his statements play fast and loose with Scripture. He twists the meaning to the point of torturing it.

Because of DuPlessis' emphasis on ecumenism, he was asked to turn in his pastoral credentials from the Assembly of God in 1962. Even that group had the wherewithal to see that DuPlessis was going seriously off the path biblically. He never left the Assemblies of God denomination and twenty years later, his pastoral credentials were returned to him.

---

[9] https://churchwatchcentral.com/2017/05/06/resource-what-is-the-nar/ (12/20/2017)

In 1961, DuPlessis became a member of the godless *World Council of Churches*, whose main push was toward ecumenism.[10] One of his articles that also pushed ecumenism was published in 1977 in *Vision Magazine*. This was an Australian New Order of Latter Rain (NOLR) publication (which evolved into the Charismatic Movement) from Alan Langstaff. The article was titled, "The Renewal of Christianity – It Must Be Both, Charismatic and Ecumenical."

DuPlessis' reasoning is a mix of Scripture-twisting and odd thinking as he wrote to prove that God has always been in favor of ecumenism. He attempted to show that this is what Jesus meant, that eventually His disciples and apostles adopted this thinking and that ultimately, the church can only be blessed when it fully embraces the spirit of ecumenism.

DuPlessis' article is a rambling, incoherent treatise on why ecumenism is God's way. Here are several quotes from the article:

"*In the beginning of His ministry, 'Jesus sent forth twelve, and commanded them, saying, Go not into the way of the Gentiles, and into any city of the Samaritans enter ye not: But go rather to the lost sheep of the house of Israel. And as ye go, preach, saying, The kingdom of heaven is at hand. Heal the sick, cleanse the lepers, raise the dead, cast out devils; freely ye have received, freely give.' (Matthew 10:5-8). What a powerful Gospel with signs following. But, is it possible? For Jews only? not for Gentiles and Samaritans? In modern times Jesus would be labelled 'racist' and 'sectarian.' Yet, soon He changed, and showed a strong ecumenical spirit, for He prophesied: (See Matthew 24:3-14), 'And this Gospel of the kingdom shall be preached in all the world for a witness unto all nations, and then shall the end come.' Thus the end-time must be a time for the whole human family to be reached by the charismatic message, or by the Gospel preached in the power of the Holy Ghost with signs following.*"[11]

This is the normal thinking for many within NAR, the idea that the gospel of the kingdom exceeds the gospel of salvation and is fulfilled in the drive toward ecumenism. This is exactly why many within NAR can couple with people from the world (including the New Age) in order to bring about the same purpose.

DuPlessis praised the creation of Israel, which is noteworthy. However, he also praised the creation of the World Council of Churches by stating, "Another great event in 1948 was the founding of the World

---

10 https://churchwatchcentral.com/2016/08/23/charismatic-leaders-destroying-christianity-since-1948/ (12/20/2017)

11 Vision Magazine 25, 1977, article by David J.DuPlessis (emphasis in original)

Council of Churches in Amsterdam, in an attempt by Protestantism to become more *ecumenical.*"[12]

Throughout this one article, DuPlessis condemns denominationalism as opposing God's plan. He taught that as the churches became more denominational, they rejected Charismata. In effect, he referred to these churches as *schisms* that ultimately became dead orthodoxy.

Ultimately, DuPlessis claims that the reason the Church is so weak is because of its failure to understand the Eucharist fully. If we truly understood the purpose of the Eucharist (according to DuPlessis), we would have a more forgiving and therefore, ecumenical spirit among Christians. This would work in God's favor as it would prepare the world for the return of Jesus.

"*Some danger signals are lately appearing in the Charismatic Movement. One of the most outstanding characteristics of the movement had been its ecumenicity, in the prayer groups and fellowships. Members of all churches and confessions were welcome and there was no questions asked about church membership. Neither was there any attack on, or criticism of, the churches. The Spirit of love, or more correctly the fruit of the Spirit – love, joy, peace, long-suffering, gentleness, goodness, faith, meekness, and temperance — was so fresh and rich in the lives of prayer group leaders and participants, that forgiveness triumphed over all differences, both cultural and traditional.*"[13]

DuPlessis also seems to completely ignore the true meaning of the text in some cases. Where God mentions His Spirit, DuPlessis states that the word refers to *Charismata.* In fact, in the Old Testament, either the Hebrew word *pneuma* or *ruach* would have been used.

"*Joel tells us that God said: 'I will pour out of my spirit (charismatic), upon all flesh, (ecumenical).' No government or ecclesial authority can prevent this or stop God's action.*"[14]

The way in which DuPlessis erroneously defines and applies God's Word to both the Charismatic Movement and ecumenism is patently absurd and proves a complete lack of integrity. The man was obviously directed by a spirit which was *not* from God. Had I understood what he was teaching during my involvement in the Charismatic Movement, I would have left it sooner. DuPlessis' viewpoints are simply blasphemous,

---

[12] Ibid (emphasis in original)
[13] Vision Magazine 25, 1977, article by David J.DuPlessis (emphasis in original)
[14] Ibid (Emphasis in original)

and there is no other way to label it. Ecumenism is really the "spirit of Babel" or Babylon, but this reasoning has continued as part of NAR.

NAR proponents also firmly believe that God has anointed new "apostles" *today*. This is the case with late C. Peter Wagner, whom many credit as being the unofficial leader of today's NAR movement. Wagner stood on the platform at the Lakeland Revival where Todd Bentley was "anointed" as an apostle and stated that there were 500 apostles today and Bentley was joining them.

Interestingly enough, Church Watch Central notes that Wagner separated Christianity from NAR, "*claiming [NAR is] the fastest growing religion/movement right next to Islam.*"[15] This was likely offered to support the notion that NAR is approved by God and is proved by the tremendous growth and overall numbers. Do numbers really matter where God is concerned? It is not *quantity* that counts, but *quality* that means anything and makes the supreme difference in the lives of people.

Regarding the idea of apostles today, in its most general usage, all Christians are "apostles" because we are "sent ones," which is what the word means. Fitted by the indwelling Holy Spirit to evangelize the lost and spread the gospel (Matthew 28), we are *sent* into the world for this express purpose. However, NAR believes that God is still appointing and anointing "prophets" and "apostles" today who have the same authority that God bestowed on the original prophets and apostles of old.

Leaders within NAR say that the God who worked miracles in the past, by giving prophetic voice and special authority to those previously marked and called by Him, is now giving that same voice and authority to others today. Jesus' apostles in the gospels and the book of Acts were forerunners for what God intended to do *now*. Therefore, God is still working in that manner today. What this ultimately means is that God is still writing His Word, though not with pen and paper, but with prophetic "voices." This is decidedly New Age; therefore, it is demonic.

Either what NAR leaders teach and what people experience is biblical, or it is not. There can be no middle ground, and God's Word *must* be used to determine whether the things seen and heard within NAR are biblical. If instead of being used, God's Word is set aside, then that leaves only *subjectivity* to determine truthfulness. However, we cannot leave it up to subjectivity. There is tremendous danger in that.

---

[15] https://churchwatchcentral.com/2017/05/06/resource-what-is-the-nar/ (12/20/2017)

There are numerous videos on the internet highlighting the *Voice of the Apostles Conference* held on October 17-20, 2017, in Lancaster, PA. Viewers see and hear NAR leaders pray over people who are going to be anointed as pastors and teachers within NAR. Simply search for *Voice of the Apostles Conference* on YouTube to see what comes up. Take some time to view some of those videos in their entirety, if possible.

I have watched many videos from this conference and what is seen is either of God, self, or Satan. In one particular video (see link below[16]) NAR leaders prepare to "anoint" people for service within NAR. These people stand behind NAR leaders on the platform.

Some individuals can be seen twitching and experiencing other involuntary movements as NAR leaders pray over them. As the camera pans across the stage, we see several people start to literally whip their heads from side-to-side. No one seems concerned.

Eventually, people start to fall over backward as though God is knocking them over like bowling pins. This same type of thing often happens at Benny Hinn gatherings, where he might wave his coat jacket at people, do some exaggerated arm and hand movement like a magician, or blow on them. As a point of interest, Benny Hinn was also one of the speakers at *Voice of the Apostles Conference.*

As I viewed one of the videos from this event, I was startled to see something rather frightening happen. At one point, a woman fell to the floor of the stage and began writhing and *screaming.* Her scream sounds as if she is in absolute dread.

I know of no occurrence in Scripture where the Holy Spirit manifested Himself through a *believer* who screamed in response to the indwelling. The man who caught the screaming woman at the conference was rather shaken and did not quite know what to do in response. NAR leaders surrounded her and continued praying for her. Her screaming continued. This was supposedly God manifesting Himself?

These videos are filled with example after example of people twitching, shaking, making strange sounds, falling to the floor as if experiencing epileptic fits, and more. Quite honestly, it appears as though some of what these people are experiencing is quite scary for them.

Cackling laughter can be heard as well. I have a difficult time crediting God with any of this because the Bible does not appear to support it. NAR leaders seem completely undisturbed by these events.

---

[16] https://www.youtube.com/watch?v=EPD7W9sXao4 (12/20/2017)

It is also interesting to note that during the *Voice of the Apostles Conference*, NAR leaders who walk on stage to pray over these people do several things. They, of course, lay hands on those who are to be anointed for ministry. They also lean into them and blow on or kiss them. They move their arms and hands in large flourishes of movement with recipients falling to the floor, shaking, or making other involuntary movements or sounds.

During the course of one of the videos, the main NAR leader turns to the audience and announces *his* blessing on them (he says, "*I bless the people standing...*"). He does not wish *God's* blessing on them. He is actually giving *his* blessing. Of course, he ends his prayer in the Name of Jesus, but this leader – as a NAR apostle – believes he is extending his blessing to these people. The level of arrogance within NAR is astounding.

What the people on stage in the video were experiencing appears to be very similar to something in the Occult and New Age. It is called the *kundalini awakening*. Those who teach this awakening say that it should never be done without at least some prior knowledge of what will occur, and never without an instructor who is well versed in the process itself and can oversee it as it unfolds. There are dangers in going it alone.

By the way, this *kundalini awakening*, according to the mystery religions, is the awakening of the *divinity* within the person. It is the first step toward *self-actualization* toward reaching our divine potential.

There are many other videos (see links below[17], [18]) on the internet that allow us to compare what happened at the *Voice of the Apostles Conference* with what occurs when New Age, Buddhist, Hindu, or other pagan practitioners go through a *kundalini awakening*. The process is eerily similar to what occurred at the *Voice of the Apostles Conference.*

If readers choose to view the myriad of kundalini awakening videos, you will notice the various contortions, movements, and sounds associated with this awakening. The people in the videos that are experiencing this awakening are all moving involuntarily. Pay close attention to that.

Other videos highlight what are known as "kriyas" in Hinduism, Buddhism, and the New Age.[19] "*Kriya refers to the outward physical expression of awakened kundalini and look like spontaneous yoga*

---

[17] https://www.youtube.com/watch?v=bsetpxZWpgA (12/20/2017)
[18] https://www.youtube.com/watch?v=Cxryti-T4KA (12/20/2017)
[19] https://www.youtube.com/watch?v=zCQFSwkvwUc (12/20/2017)

postures."[20] Were the people on the platform at the *Voice of the Apostles Conference* actually experiencing kriyas and *not* the manifestation of the Holy Spirit? It is a very real possibility.

By the way, this alleged *kundalini awakening* starts at the base of the spine, travels up the spine through numerous "chakras" and ends at the pineal gland (also known as the third eye, located in our brains). The final stage of the awakening is the opening of the pineal gland. Once open, it is said to give one a window into the spiritual dimension and access one's inner divinity.

People who go through this awakening say they become much more sensitive to the spirit world. People also claim to begin hearing voices and seeing visions as they become more attuned to the spiritual realm.

The Bible warns us to avoid this type of divination. It is abhorrent to the Lord and offers nothing good to the practitioner. Those Christians who seek a type of kundalini awakening (even if it is claimed to be "Christian") are opening themselves up to demonic activity, a world God never intended us to experience and know. It is another way for Satan to entice Christians into the area of the forbidden.

According to proponents of NAR, the experiences associated with their anointings are credited as the working of the Holy Spirit. If so, we again need to ask why it seems to happen within the pagan religions in the exact same way?

While it might be argued that Satan has counterfeited the Holy Spirit, can that really be the case? *Kundalini awakening* has been around long before the Holy Spirit gave birth to the Church in the first century and long before God began manifesting Himself within members of the Church, Christ's Body. Is it possible that the same power behind occult *kundalini awakening* is the same power behind the experiences at the *Voice of the Apostles* conferences?

Why do people think they need this? Do the experiences actually bring them closer to God? Are the experiences themselves accepted as being from God because they sometimes seem pleasurable? Do these experiences create more of the fruit of the Holy Spirit? That is certainly one of the tests that should be applied to the experience.

Watching videos where it appears that people have lost control of themselves would indicate that what they are experiencing is *not* the fruit of the Spirit at all. Self-control is part of His fruit.

---

[20] http://www.ourlightbody.com/index.php/part-iii-human-metamorphosis/chapter-6-all-about-kundalini/what-are-kundalini-kriyas (12/20/2017)

There are people, as noted, who appear terrified during their personal experiences. Is that also a characteristic of the fruit of the Holy Spirit? Certainly not.

People who go through *kundalini awakening* tell of extreme feelings of love, peace, and acceptance upon the awakening. Those who experience this feel greater love for others. The dividing walls (of theological and doctrinal differences) come down, and they begin to see all people as part of the brotherhood and sisterhood of humanity. *Personal experience*, not God's Word, becomes their own truth barometer based on how they *feel* about something.

What is telling about the results of these experiences is that the "love" felt by the practitioner toward others always results in allowing people to believe whatever seems good to them to believe. In other words, those who have gone through *kundalini awakening* feel no need to critique or analyze another person's beliefs, but simply accept them as truth. It all results in a huge love fest where people are simply embraced, regardless of their beliefs.

Is that what Jesus did? Certainly He loved people far better than we can love anyone; however, that same love drove Him to point out the error in other people's lives. Jesus did that for what purpose? So that people could be *saved*. To simply "love" people (feel great about them) does absolutely nothing and the lost remain lost.

Recall when Jesus brought Peter back into the fold. This took place after Peter denied Jesus multiple times on the night of Jesus' betrayal. After that incident, Peter went out and wept bitterly. Later, after Jesus rose from the dead, He specifically asked Peter three times if Peter loved Him. Peter responded that He did. Each time after Peter's response, Jesus said, "*Feed my sheep*" (*John 21:17*).

Jesus' words imply that Peter had a job to do. Peter was called to love people, and if he really loved them, he would be willing to tell them the truth. This biblical truth is what "feeds" people.

Jesus told his disciples that He had "food" they were not aware of and it was to do the will of Him who sent Jesus *(John 4:34)*. Peter was to "feed" Jesus' sheep by presenting biblical truth to them that would cause them to grow to spiritual maturity and a deeper faith in Christ.

Exactly what "truth" is gained by Christians who undergo some sort of ecstatic experience? Have they become more mature in Christ? How so, if there was no tangible biblical truth taught to them?

What about truth as expressed in God's Word? Are we no longer to be concerned about false teachers and erroneous doctrine, as Jesus, Paul, Peter, John, and others were during their day? If not, why not? What has changed? Is it possible that Christians are starting to chase after things that make them feel good while ignoring their actual responsibility to spread the gospel and live a life that pleases God and brings Him glory?

Many so-called Christian conferences, churches, and gatherings now teach that Christians need to set aside differences and simply embrace one another for the sake of unity. The gaps between theology and doctrine should not keep us from worshipping together and loving one another.

The problem with this type of thinking is that it dismisses much of the New Testament warnings about contending for the faith. It implies that we should not "correct" another Christian who may be in error. To do so means to be judgmental and unloving, which leads to division.

Preaching in a well-known Word of Faith church, the late Anglican Bishop Tony Palmer stated, "*diversity is divine, but division is diabolical.*" The audience responded with clapping and cheers. Palmer was wrong and understands that now since his passing. *You*, however, do not have to wait until you die to learn the truth because it is clearly expressed in God's Word. The difficulty many Christians have today is an unwillingness to spend time in God's Word – reading, studying, and memorizing it.

Jesus' ministry is proof that Palmer is wrong. Jesus' words constantly divided truth from error – the sheep from the goats. It still does this today. Jesus Himself said He came to bring a sword, not peace *(Matthew 10:34).* Jesus is also called the Prince of Peace. How then should we understand His words?

Clearly, He was intent on separating truth from falsehoods; and those who continued to pursue falsehoods saw Jesus as divisive, an enemy, someone who needed to *die*. Conversely, those who came to Jesus and embraced what He taught would find eternal peace with God, though not necessarily with other human beings. Apparently, leaders of NAR would like us to believe that persecution down through the ages was and is the result of Christians who are too pharisaical and dogmatic in their beliefs.

As noted previously, Paul says the preaching of the cross is foolishness to those who are perishing *(I Corinthians 1:18).* The world will ridicule and condemn as their eyes remain closed to the truth about Jesus. We, however, are called to love the lost with our words and actions. We are not to back away from sharing the truth. Souls hang in the eternal balance.

Parents, do you ever take the time to correct and/or discipline your children or do you only "love" them in spite of the things they do wrong?

I contend that if you never correct your children, you do not actually love them. You love *yourself* and do not want your children to dislike you. You choose to never risk it by disciplining them.

Here are some questions to consider. First, did Jesus or the apostles ever correct or rebuke those who were in error? Did they do this because they *hated* the person or because they *loved* them? Second, how is love defined by people who say we are only to love and never correct? How is love defined in God's Word? Third, is there ever a time when we are to offer correction to other Christians or is it always judgmental to do so? Fourth, if correcting someone, or contending for the faith is never a good thing, then why does Jude tell us to always contend *earnestly* for the faith *(v. 3)*? The implication is that we are to contend against *error*.

Regarding the many ecstatic experiences claimed to be of God today, what about the use of *discernment*? Should we even concern ourselves with discernment anymore? Are we to use discernment in seeking God or should we rather throw caution to the wind and trust that God would only let us experience what is good for us?

Every person has a "source" they look to as their final authority. If it is not the Bible, then it is something else, and unfortunately, for a growing number of people, their final authority is themselves. For Christians, it is to be the Scriptures alone. In them is truth.

CHAPTER 4 Growing Ecumenical Deception: Continued March Toward Romanism

Prior to his untimely death from injuries sustained in a motorcycle accident in 2014, Anglican Bishop Tony Palmer served as an unofficial liaison between the Roman Catholic Church (RCC) and Protestant denominations. His goal was to bring about a unity he felt was absent but very much needed within Christendom. He stated and believed that "*diversity is divine, but division is diabolical.*" Pope Francis considered Palmer a good influence.

Readers will recall that in the last chapter I highlighted several portions of an article written by David J. DuPlessis ("Mr. Pentecost") that supported his belief that God is all about ecumenism. He literally pleaded with Christians to embrace this move he credited as being from God, the Holy Spirit. Ecumenism is a belief that tends to undergird every movement of the Spirit since the 1906 Azusa Street Revival.

Many people believe that the Roman Catholic Church has been behind these movements either directly or indirectly because it is too coincidental that so many evangelical Christian leaders have eventually come out in support of at least aspects of Roman Catholicism. It cannot simply be chance that causes this to occur.

DuPlessis referred to Pope XXIII in glowing terms, who was so intent on doing everything he could to move Christendom toward ecumenism that he created a special department within the Vatican for that purpose.

"Then Pope John XXIII sounded the need for the *renewal* of the Church in order to *achieve* unity...More than anyone else he shook his own church to a glorious awakening, as well as all Christianity. This Saintly Pope of our times was so dedicated to the *unity* of the Church that he created, right in the Vatican, The Secretariat for Promoting Christian Unity...In this way, the Holy-Spirit was able to move within the R.C. Church, and in "the now" worldwide Catholic Charismatic Renewal, that has become the great wonder of Christianity in this age... However, I discover some agitation against this."[21]

[21] Vision Magazine 25, 1977, article by David J. DuPlessis (emphasis in original)

One can only wonder if this "agitation" that DuPlessis notes had anything to do with the great gulf that exists between Roman Catholic doctrine and that of mainline Protestantism. Of course, DuPlessis preferred to believe that this agitation was solely due to a form of "nationalism" that exists within the various denominations. This, he stated, resulted in dead formalism and elevated tradition, which of course, gave rise to a...*Pharisee mindset.*

It is clear that from the creation of the World Council of Churches to the present, each Pope has been actively pursuing unity between Catholicism and Protestantism and lately, even reaching out to Islam as well. Interestingly enough, as we will continue to see, NAR has been working to achieve this union too.

The word "catholic" means *universal.* However, the Roman Catholic Church, by the addition of the word "Roman" *limits* that universality. In spite of this fact, the Roman Catholic belief is that the true Church – Christ's Bride – is actually *their* church, the Roman Catholic Church.

In spite of the truth regarding whether or not the apostle Peter ever went to Rome and started a church there, the continued belief is that Peter was the first pope in Rome. Since Jesus said that "upon this rock," (referring to Peter's *faith*, not Peter himself; *Matthew 16:18*), Christ would build His Church, Roman Catholics believe that Jesus meant that He would establish Peter as the first pope and build the church from him. Anyone who is *not* part of the Roman Catholic Church then, is not part of the true Church, according to Roman Catholic reasoning.

Of course, Ephesians 2:19-21 tells the real story of the foundation of the Church.

"*Therefore you are no longer strangers and foreigners, but fellow citizens of the saints and members of God's household, built on the foundation of the apostles and prophets, with Christ Jesus Himself as the cornerstone. In Him the whole building is fitted together and grows into a holy temple in the Lord...*"

Clearly, the Church rests on the foundation of *all* the apostles, not simply Peter. But most importantly, Jesus Himself is the Chief Cornerstone. It is also interesting to note that the apostles will judge the tribes of Israel *(Matthew 19:28).*

Since its inception, the Roman Catholic Church has done everything in its power to be the only dominant religion. This was successfully accomplished for hundreds of years by squelching people's ability to gain personal access to the Bible. Since the Bible was not originally written in the vernacular, keeping laypeople from the Bible was not difficult.

The Roman Catholic hierarchy kept God's Word sequestered to keep the average Catholic from *misunderstanding* Scripture, which could cause them to embrace incorrect doctrine. When Luther, Calvin, Tyndale, Wycliffe, and others attempted to break from Catholic doctrine that did not align with Scriptures, there was great resistance from the Roman Catholic hierarchy.

This attempt at *reforming* abject error within Catholicism led to severe persecution and even martyrdom for those who deigned to speak against errant Catholic teachings. The Reformation made one thing very clear – salvation is by grace alone, through faith alone, in Christ alone – exactly as the Bible teaches.

Much within Roman Catholicism *continues* to pervert the biblical doctrine of salvation. It causes Roman Catholics to believe that they must partner with God to *gain* and *maintain* their salvation or they may very well lose it. This is merely one sad reality of Romanism. At best, Roman Catholicism teaches that all will partake of Purgatory for a time, with some spending more time there than others. This is not a biblical doctrine, but one based on extra-biblical writings and the traditional beliefs of the Roman Catholic Church.

The Bible teaches that salvation is a completely free gift of God. There is absolutely nothing anyone can do to earn it *(Ephesians 2:8-10)*, and we cannot lose it *(Romans 8)*, though we most certainly can lose potential rewards *(I Corinthians 3:12)*. For a greater awareness of actual doctrine and theology taught by the Roman Catholic Church, readers may wish to obtain a copy of the *Catechism of the Catholic Church* to add to their reference library.

It would appear that a massive push is underway to bring more people (back) into Roman Catholicism. This is the end goal of all ecumenical efforts, including those which occurred in the Charismatic Movement through today with NAR.

As noted, Catholics will tell you that theirs is the true Church, the church universal that God is building and they trace their roots to Acts 2. I was recently reminded of this belief by a reader of my blog who happens to be Catholic and took umbrage with some of the remarks made in a past article there. Like this reader, Catholics in general staunchly believe that the Roman Catholic Church is *the* Church and changing their minds on this point is difficult at best.

Interestingly enough, in his speech before Kenneth Copeland's congregation, Tony Palmer said much the same thing. He also lambasted the fact that there are so many different denominations within Christendom, stating the number of separate denominations is above 33,000. It is easy to group all factions of Christendom together as though they are merely denominations. People who do so normally include all *cults* and *sects* with other, more mainline Protestant denominations. Scientology, Jehovah's Witnesses, Mormonism, Christian Science, and many others like them are decidedly *not* Christian, based on their own peculiar doctrinal beliefs when compared with Scripture. Most of these cults deny the full deity of Jesus, preferring to accept Him simply as a "god" but not the only God Almighty. There are many other differences, and as stated previously, most of these cults use Christian verbiage to explain their own doctrines, which simply adds to the confusion.

Many of the differences from one true denomination to another have nothing to do with the actual fundamentals of the faith (the Deity of Christ, the virgin birth, etc.). Issues such as how often to participate in the Lord's Supper, styles of worship, which version of the Bible to use, etc., are the main disagreements. In those cases, people seek out a denomination that works for them, while not disavowing the main fundamentals of Christianity.

Remember, the Charismatic Movement came out of the New Order of Latter Rain (NOLR) in the mid-1950s, in Saskatchewan, Canada. What is also very interesting about NOLR is that "*...at its inception, it was pushing the Apostolic Governance heresy, Unity Power heresy and ecumenism with the pagan Roman Catholic Church.*"[22] Again, this was in 1948, roughly eighty years ago. Where are we today?

I recall from my own involvement in the Charismatic Movement the fact that many Roman Catholics worshipped and gathered together with us (Protestants). At the time it was inspiring because we all thought it was great that people of different "denominations" could come together to worship the same God. This simply proved my lack of biblical knowledge and understanding. The point is not that we avoid people we disagree with. In II Corinthians 6:14, Paul asks how light and dark can worship together? Clearly, the differences in doctrine and theology between Roman Catholicism and evangelical Protestantism are wide. How is it possible to bring both together, so that true worship is achieved?

---

[22] Vision Magazine 25, 1977, article by David J. DuPlessis

In the Charismatic Movement, neither doctrine nor theology mattered much since everyone was simply trying to draw closer to God and "catch the wave" of what He was doing in the world. At times, the speakers at the Full Gospel Businessman's meetings were Roman Catholic. I never really paid attention. I was simply there to get more of God. How immature and self-centered.

Today, many evangelical leaders are adopting aspects of Catholic liturgy and introducing them to their own congregations. This is becoming the norm.

More and more people are reaching across the aisle and embracing aspects of Roman Catholicism. Yet Catholic doctrine has not experienced a noticeable change. Catholics believe that salvation must be at least maintained (if not *gained* altogether) by the penitent or they will risk losing it. Some form of the system of indulgences comes up at every Catholic funeral. You can still pray or buy a deceased person's spirit out of Purgatory.

Due to its reliance on Augustinian writings, Roman Catholicism often interprets eschatological passages of Scripture (those having to do with future events) *allegorically*, as opposed to interpreting the text literally (in its most plain and ordinary sense).

What does this do to the text of Scripture? Obviously, it changes the intended meaning of God's Word and often does so in a dramatic way. Because the Roman Catholic Church adopted Augustine's theology, this method of interpretation is passed down to each new generation of Catholics. It is simply heard, believed, and accepted.

Like Muslims in Islam, the average Catholic is simply *told* what the Bible means from the *Augustinian* perspective, the official viewpoint of Roman Catholicism. Augustine was intent on moving Christianity away from Judaism, and because of that, he had a tendency to throw out the baby with the bathwater in numerous instances.

Because of that approach, passages of Scripture that refer to God's reinstatement of Israel in the last days are instead applied to the Church. Of course, in that context, the Church equals the Roman Catholic Church. This is, of course, why the Pope often sides against Israel and the Jews there. For those who understand the Bible allegorically, the Church has fully *replaced* Israel. Therefore Israel's presence in the Middle East is first, an anomaly, and second, an unnecessary thorn in the flesh to Arabs.

Protestants, however, understand the Church as the Body of Christ, a *spiritual* "building" that God is constructing with each new person who becomes saved. For the Roman Catholic, there is no salvation outside of the Roman Catholic Church, so Catholicism represents the true Church. If you become a member of Catholicism as an adult (or through infant baptism), you are saved automatically because you have become part of the Roman Catholic Church. It works the same way in Islam for Muslims as well, but that is not what the Bible teaches.

There are many differences between Catholicism and Protestantism. Space does not permit an in-depth consideration of these differences here, and it is beyond this book's intended purview. Catholics are taught to believe that Roman Catholicism *is* the Church and to remain outside of it is to remain *unsaved*. It is interesting that this belief within Catholicism is not seen as judgmental or divisive.

For Protestants, because the mainline denominations are often very similar, a person can belong to a Baptist church or a Presbyterian church and be saved in either one. However, simply to become a member of a Protestant denomination does not equal salvation. For most, a person must be saved first and must provide testimony of that before they can become a member of a local body.

Increasingly, Protestants are being invited to return to the Roman Catholic Church or lose out. Again, though this would be seen as divisive if someone from a Protestant denomination made or intimated that statement, it is not seen that way when the Pope says it. Why? Because Catholics believe the Pope is an *apostle* and when he speaks, he speaks the mind of God. Catholics do not see the need to use discernment because this is what they have always known and they simply accept without question.

The same applies to many people within the Charismatic Movement and NAR. There is a great need for discernment. The things that pass as Christian doctrine within NAR churches and gatherings leave a great deal to be desired. But they also have their "apostles" too, which implies that they also speak for God or speak God's mind. So, if NAR pushes ecumenism, as the Pope has pushed it since the two groups agree, then it truly must be God's mind, right? But the Bible is rarely if ever considered. When it *is* used, it is used like piecemeal with verses here or there torn from their context to buttress a particular teaching, even though if left in its original context, it would likely negate that particular viewpoint.

The tagline for the Kairos 2017 Conference was *Unity + Revival Conference 2017*. This conference was designed to bring about unity between various denominations *and* Roman Catholicism. The goal was to set aside differences that have come to the fore since the Reformation and simply embrace one another. The question must be asked, what has changed within Catholicism *since* the Reformation? If Luther were alive today, would he no longer have difficulties with Catholic theology?

I believe that this push toward unity/ecumenism is ultimately moving global society toward the things that will grow into place as we approach the end of this age – a one-world religious system and a one-world government. It will eventually incorporate all aspects of religion, including NAR and the New Age movement. It could very well all unite under the auspices of the Roman Catholic Church. That is a very distinct possibility as many of these movements since the early 1900s have endeavored to grasp hands with Roman Catholicism.

The Bible highlights the fact that there will be an Antichrist – "the final man of sin" as Paul refers to him in 2 Thessalonians 2. This Antichrist will oppose all that God is and will seek to raise himself up as being equal to God. His lying signs and wonders will capture the hearts and minds of people across the globe.

We can also expect to see a False Prophet who will direct attention and accolades *toward* the Antichrist. Of course, we will not know who these individuals are until they arrive on the scene and are revealed, but certainly many have offered their guesses. I have no interest in attempting to guess.

What is most interesting is if the Antichrist walked onto the religious scene today, he would likely be fully accepted and even worshipped by many with the New Age, NAR, and quite possibly, Roman Catholic Church movements. Why is this? It is due to a complete lack of discernment on the part of many. This coming Antichrist will be so powerfully indwelt by Satan himself that because of the signs and wonders he will be enabled to perform, the entire world will follow him.

"*The coming of the lawless one is by the activity of Satan with all power and false signs and wonders, and with all wicked deception for those who are perishing, because they refused to love the truth and so be saved. Therefore God sends them a strong delusion, so that they may believe what is false, in order that all may be condemned who did not believe the truth but had pleasure in unrighteousness.*" *(2 Thessalonians 2:9-12)*

"*They worshiped the dragon who had given authority to the beast, and they worshipped the beast, saying, 'Who is like the beast, and who can wage war against it?*'" *(Revelation 13:4)*

This future leader will capture the fascination of the world. He will enthrall the world with supernatural signs and wonders. Because people will prefer truth to lies, God will provide a strong delusion so that they will give themselves completely over the lies of the Antichrist. God will do this because they had no "pleasure in righteousness." (*2 Thessalonians 2:10-23*). This is what is happening in the world today with movements like NAR.

Leaders within NAR teach that signs and wonders are of God and should be accepted without question. People are being trained to learn to expect the Presence of God through these various manifestations. Because of this, there is no need to read the Bible and study it, and there is certainly no reason to memorize it. God is doing something new that is not in His Word. If you want to be "with it" and "hip" to what God is doing, set your Bible aside and follow the leadings of NAR leaders and the alleged leading of the Holy Spirit.

Since 1948, it has been disconcerting to see the exponential growth that has resulted from this push toward "unity." A larger leap took place in the 1970s, and still another huge push in the 1990s. It is now 2018 and the latest group to carry the baton is NAR – the New Apostolic Reformation. They preach not Christ crucified, but signs and wonders. It does not matter what you believe. Just come and *experience* God manifesting Himself to you as NAR leaders impart one "anointing" after another onto unsuspecting, yet culpable people.

Why is there such a dearth of discernment today? It is because people do not read the Bible. They do not study it on their own within its own context and framework.

More often than not, if Christians open God's Word at all today, they do so once a week. NAR has done its work. People today prefer to chase *experiences.* They want to feel good about themselves and others. For that to happen, doctrinal barriers must come down.

Brothers and sisters, we have an obligation to live in a way that brings God great glory. Too much of what is out there simply glorifies the flesh, not God.

CHAPTER 5 New Age, Dominionism, and NAR: Common Bonds

I've written numerous articles dealing with Dominionism in the past. They can be found at *www.studygrowknowblog.com* by doing a search in the search box at the top right. Simply type in the word "*dominionism*" and hit "enter." The results will bring up the articles. We have also dealt with numerous aspects of the New Age movement and to gain access to those, simply use the same procedure as described above by using the search term "*New Age.*"

There is some crossover with Dominionism and NAR because of NAR theology (such as it is). Each of these areas has its own unique outlook, which attracts different types of people to each one. However, what might not be so readily seen, is how alike all three areas – *New Age*, *Dominionisn*, and *NAR* – are when we take a closer look under the hood, so to speak.

There is actually one very important thing that ties each of these separate groups together. As the end of this age draws to a close, these three separate groups will likely end up becoming far more cohesive and unified. I can see a time when they might actually come together unofficially, if not officially, because of the ideology they share. I am *not* saying that from any sense of the "prophetic," but simply because of how things appear to be moving in society with these three groups.

What is that one thing that will create the bridge between these groups? It is nothing less than the return of the Christ. Let me clarify that please, because I am not referring to God the Son, Jesus, who will return at the very end of this age to close the Tribulation period, after which He will judge the sheep and the goats and begin setting up His Millennial Kingdom. No, I'm talking about another "Christ," an impostor, who will gain the attention of the world and be seen and accepted as the long-awaited "messiah," and who will ultimately be worshiped as though God *(2 Thessalonians 2)*, as we previously noted. Scripture tells us that prior to the return of the real Jesus, an impostor who will be *the* Antichrist will have his day. It will essentially be Satan's last attempt to imitate and replace God as he promised to do so long ago *(Isaiah 14:14).* Of course, Satan will fail miserably because he is *not* God.

We need to remember that God Himself will allow all of this to occur for His purposes and glory. As this age draws to a close just prior to Jesus' physical return, the gulf between righteousness and evil will become extremely obvious, at least for those who have not become deceived and deluded in their thinking.

However, when the Antichrist is revealed, everyone will be either for the Antichrist or against him. It does not appear from the Bible that there will be any fence sitters.

We know that the New Age has been looking for – yearning for and working for – the coming of the *Maitreya*, the New Age term for *Messiah*. The New Age has been teaching of the growing "Christ consciousness" that is dawning throughout the earth.

What is most important for New Agers is that this consciousness continues to grow and impact society throughout the globe, ultimately creating a unity among society that has not heretofore existed (at least since the Tower of Babel in Genesis 11). Many within the New Age speak of the *cosmic* energy of the coming "Christ." They believe that as people unite in purpose, fully focused and working to bring this "Christ" to earth (they tell us our "energy" and "thoughts" are capable of doing that), this Christ will finally appear.

Benjamin Creme worked most of his adult life to bring "Christ" (Maitreya), to earth. This "Christ" will rule over the coming Age of Aquarius (or the Aquarian Shift), which is said to bring the utopia they believe will occur on this earth. However, first, there will be much travail as the world shifts from the current Piscean Age to the coming Aquarian Age.

Of course, no one knows when this shift will take place, but one of the things that will occur with this shift will be the "Christ's" coming to earth. This is what the New Age teaches (in very general terms). In essence, the coming "Christ" (Maitreya) is hindered only because of the shift that needs to occur.

Dominionism, like the New Age, is made up of people who are often part of Christendom, or the visible Church (which contains both authentic believers and professing believers). However, Dominionists can be clearly seen as Christian. For someone to believe in Dominionism, they must embrace forms of religion and acknowledge at the very least, a higher power that controls and oversees life on this planet. In that sense, Dominionism is similar to New Age thought.

Of course, Dominionism is far more outwardly expressed in specifically Christian terminology. The New Age also uses Christian-sounding terminology, but often it is only to hide their true meaning.

Christian Dominionists believe that the God of the Bible desires Christians to rise to power through societal systems currently in place, like politics/government, family, education, the arts, etc. This is so that His Word might then effectively govern the nation.

The belief that America is a Christian nation is sometimes called *soft dominionism.* The idea that God wants only Christians to hold government offices and run the country according to biblical law is called *hard dominionism.*

As noted above, Dominionists believe they must work to recreate society by taking control of it through elected office, education, the arts, etc., (the Seven Mountain Mandate). Hardcore Dominionist beliefs ultimately lead to Reconstructionism and Kingdom Now Theology. The former includes people who believe that it is the Christian's responsibility to take control of the world in their particular gifted area or calling until the entirety of the world is *subdued.*

Kingdom Now advocates normally include Charismatics, Pentecostals, and people from NAR. They believe that Christians are to take control of the world and subdue it through *spiritual warfare.* This is one reason why signs, wonders, and manifestations of God's Presence are such a big deal with NAR. This is how spiritual warfare is accomplished. In either camp, once the world has been "subdued," Jesus will be able to return and rule.

Both groups, New Age and those within Dominionism, believe that they must do all they can to bring forth the "Christ" or Jesus. Though these groups remain aloof ideologically and theologically, they share the belief that their efforts will bring about the return of their "Messiah."

As noted, proponents of NAR are essentially Dominionist in position. In an article I wrote on my blog, "Losing Control in the Name of God,"[23] there is a video included that highlights Todd Bentley and his wife, Jessa. In front of a gathering, he invited her to explain the dream she had.

During the course of her explanation, she mentioned "*bringing God's Kingdom to earth,*" which is what Dominionists and those in NAR believe all Christians are to be about. Certainly, there are a few verses here and there, which when taken out of context might appear to teach that people on earth are in some way involved in bringing the Lord back to earth. However, when the Bible is allowed to interpret itself, no such conclusion can be seen or intelligently argued.

The plain fact of the matter is that Jesus will return at the precise time that has been previously chosen by the Godhead, in eternity past before

---

23 https://studygrowknowblog.com/2017/11/29/losing-control-in-the-name-of-god/ (12/20/2017)

the foundations of this world. Humanity plays no part in the physical return of Jesus any more than it played in His first coming.

As then, when the times had reached fulfillment, Jesus was born of a virgin. Regarding His second coming, He will come at the Father's bidding, at the precise time when things reach their fulfillment. God, not human beings, will oversee that. We have no hand in it.

Our job is to witness to the unsaved people of this world. There is no mention in Scripture of Jesus being able to return after His people have worked to change the world enough so that He *can* return.

People in NAR believe that all the manifestations evidenced in their gatherings are God speaking to us. This includes all alleged words of knowledge and prophecies given telling us that God is doing something "new." These all represent the church engaging in spiritual warfare.

The more these manifestations occur, the greater the warfare and victory. This will allegedly lead to the second coming of Jesus. This is why the phrase "*bringing God's Kingdom to earth*" is often heard within NAR and its many offshoots.

What is interesting is that most of these prophetic voices that claim the authority of God's Word always speak of *revival* and rarely anything else. This was the case during my time in the Charismatic Movement, and it is the case now.

At every meeting, I attended there would be at least one person who would stand up and "prophesy" about a new move of God. Sometimes, the speaker quoted a mishmash of Scripture, while at other times they just spoke as if God was moving them, using their own words. But it is always about revival.

I recall that some of the prophecies were fairly specific, meaning, the person might say something like, "God is doing a new thing. He is going to pour out His Spirit starting in the East and moving to the West. People will glorify the Lord in renewed strength and vigor." Often, the alleged prophecies sounded very similar.

This behavior is still common today; however none of the prophecies I recall hearing included any portion of the Gospel. God was simply going to pour out His Spirit.

On the *Charisma News* website in 2016, James Goll wrote an article[24] prophesying that God was going to do a new work. He explained how it would happen. The link at the bottom of the page will direct to read the entirety of his article, but a few key excerpts are provided below.

"*I gave this word concerning the West Coast Rumble for over a three-year period of time in multiple locations. I wrote it up on my personal ministry e-blasts and it was then partially picked up both by Charisma and the Elijah List.*

"*I always stated that I saw it beginning in San Diego, and then going to seaports up and down the entire West Coast. It started with one dream around four years ago. Later I had other dreams and expanded the word some, so as to include Tijuana, Mexico, because that was what I saw. When it goes there, it will go more into a Crusade-type mode.*"

Goll is referring to an anointing of the Lord, what he calls a "rumble." He says that once it landed in San Diego, it would continue to go up and down the West Coast and into Canada. He said he was also warned ostensibly by God not to refer to the West Coast as the "Left" Coast, "*but there will be such a move of My Spirit that it will be the Righteous Coast.*"

Goll wrote the article for *Charisma* in April of 2016, and I have not seen how the West Coast has become more "righteous," but maybe I have missed something. I have seen more *unrighteousness*, but maybe I am looking at things incorrectly.

What is often the case with Dominionists, New Agers, and NAR is this belief that people – Christians especially – should be *social justice warriors* (SJWs). This means that we should help people break the law to come to the United States illegally from Mexico and other places because those nations are more in line with third world nations. Their governments do not care about them, so Christians in the United States should reach out to them.

Consequently, America spends exorbitant amounts of tax dollars on illegal aliens and the repercussions of the crime, drugs, and anchor babies. There is nothing in Scripture that encourages Christians to break the law and support those who do so under the guise of helping humanity. However, this is often how many people think.

Reading Goll's article reminds me of just how nebulous and contrived the prophecies were that I heard during my involvement in the Charismatic

---

24 https://www.charismanews.com/opinion/56478-james-goll-s-prophesied-west-coast-rumble-hits-seattle (12/20/2017)

Movement. The emphasis is on signs and wonders, not the gospel of Jesus Christ that saves people from their sin.

"*I repeatedly saw that Jerame Nelson would be given a spearheading assignment concerning this movement of **signs and wonders where healing and miracles** will eventually become easy. I saw many leaders being anointed for such a time as this.*" *(emphasis added)*, continued Goll in the same article.

People in the New Age also believe in healing and signs and wonders. There is really not a great deal of difference. Certainly, God is quite capable of healing people, and I believe He still heals, as He chooses to do so. Yet, there were times in the Bible when He did not heal for a variety of reasons.

Goll goes onto mention Che Ahn specifically, another apostle in the NAR movement. In fact, since C. Peter Wagner's death, it is generally accepted that Ahn is the head apostle now. Ahn denies this.

"*I saw Che Ahn of HIM releasing a 'Father's Blessing' to this activity, and this has happened at the San Diego meetings. Che is one of the 'Fathers' to give a blessing to this historic period of time. This deals with the generations coming together. The Lord gave me a dream in January 2016 to: 'Keep your eyes on your sons and your daughters.' Yes, it is happening! It is generational, and it is cross-cultural, and it includes both men and women.*"

This is so tragic and so filled with hubris that it actually mocks the very nature of our Lord and Savior. It does so by elevating these individuals, making them equal in authority to the original apostles that Jesus hand-picked, including Paul. Che Ahn is going to give a "Father's" blessing at this time?

Notice also that Goll claims God gave him a dream several months prior to writing the article. God gave him the nebulous, "Watch your kids." The leaning within the Charismatic Movement has *always* depended on the fact that they have no problem with women pastors or with women speaking to mixed crowds. Paul teaches the exact opposite, and the reasons he provides are quite clear, yet just as clearly denied by women's groups and many men today. Read 1 Timothy 2:12-14 and see if you notice the two reasons Paul said women cannot exercise authority over a man.[25] The reasons are there.

---

[25] Women In the Pulpit? https://christianpublishinghouse.co/2017/01/03/women-in-the-pulpit/

Goll's alleged prophecy clearly emphasizes signs and wonders. He refers back to Azusa, to Latter Rain, to the Jesus People Movement, to "pioneers" like Aimee Semple McPherson, to Jack Hayford, and to many others. He draws a connecting line backward in an attempt to show that signs and wonders was the very thing God has been using to bring tremendous revival to America and the world.

I have to ask, to what end? Where is the Gospel? Where is the pointing out of sin and the need for repentance? Where is the preaching about the fact that the unsaved are enemies of God but that can be reconciled through repentance and salvation, otherwise known as being born again, or born from above *(John 3)*? Where is all that? It is absent because these people think that miraculous events seen in signs and wonders will simply sweep over people – whether saved or unsaved – and their lives will change for the better.

But if no one explains to a person their personal need for a Savior, how will they know? All they will know and understand is that they have *experienced* something that may have made them *feel* good. Beyond that, they do not really know exactly *what* happened.

Such is NAR today, depending upon and yearning for signs and wonders as the expression of "God among us." Rather than reading His Word, studying it, and memorizing it, these people attend conferences where the level of excitement is kicked up a few notches, and they thoroughly expect to "find" God. But again, what have they *found*?

The New Age uses essentially the same approach. They emphasize personal experiences or encounters with God. The focus is on the *experience* that is alleged to improve us by making us care more about humanity, the earth, the spirits in the spirit realm, and even aliens.

These things are common between the New Age, Dominionism, and NAR. To arrive at their particular line of reasoning, both Dominionists and NAR must set aside God's Word. They prefer the revelations gained through their various ecstatic experiences to the truth of the Bible.

All three of these groups make God out to be a liar. Through their faulty exegesis (NAR and Dominionism), and humanistic relativism (New Age), they all believe the combined efforts of humanity will play a large hand in bringing the "Christ" to earth. God speaks of a powerful delusion He will send that will overtake humanity *(II Thessalonians 2:11)*.

New Agers are already deceived and believe what is false. However, many of those within both the Dominionist and NAR camps came from evangelical churches. In essence, these people gave themselves over to deception and delusion by choice. They had the means by which to learn the truth about these false groups, but they chose to ignore that truth in favor of a religious experience.

The apostle Paul warns of the apostasy that will occur in the latter days *(II Timothy 4:3-4)*. It is my belief that we are now living in the last days. We are witnessing the unprecedented apostasy by those claiming to "live for Jesus" that we have been warned about.

What these people believe and teach is diametrically opposed to Scripture. They are dreamers and babblers; constantly presenting falsehoods eagerly adopted by those who follow them. Discernment has no place in their lives.

Those within NAR and Dominionism are now rising to attack Christians who do not see things their way. Those who disagree with NAR for instance, are considered the "Pharisees" of today, the legalists, who would squelch the alleged manifestations and moves of God.

The New Age movement also denigrates Christians and Christianity for what is perceived as our bigotry, our schisms (denominations), our legalism, and our judgmental attitudes. Of course, Christians are also condemned because we rely on Jesus only, not the pantheon of gods found within the New Age movement.

As the climax of this age occurs, those in the New Age, Dominionism, and NAR will find themselves strange bedfellows at first. However, they will likely realize that they have more in common than they ever previously understood. NAR will likely become much more New Age in its emphasis. Many people who have come out of the New Age movement only to realize that the New Age has infiltrated the visible Church have already verified this.

It simply makes sense that those in the New Age, Dominionism, and NAR will move closer toward one another (ignoring all differences in ideology), because of the common goal to bring "Christ" to earth. Yes, the world is going to worsen until Jesus returns. The Bible promises that, yet every prophecy coming out of NAR says otherwise. Whom should we believe?

A close look at Scripture tells us the world will become one in purpose and direction in the future. It will be the Tower of Babel on steroids.

At some point, according to many portions of Scripture, the world will not only become one but will then be broken up into ten regions, ruled over by ten "kings" *(Revelation 17)*. Once this occurs, the stage is set for the revealing of the Antichrist, who will rule this earth overseeing the final kingdom of the visions first seen in Daniel 2 and 7.

For the world to become one in direction and purpose, big steps are going to have to happen. As noted, New Agers refer to this coming tribulation as the birth of Aquarius. It cannot happen without travail. The result of that will be a form of peace that will convince the world the newest age has dawned; an age without war and one of true prosperity. Of course, it will all be short-lived, at least according to Scripture.

CHAPTER 6 New Age, Dominionism, and NAR: Twisted Truth

We previously focused on commonalities between the New Age, Dominionism, and New Apostolic Reformation (NAR). The one main connection is that all three of these groups believe that, due in large part to humanity's efforts, a new age will dawn leading to the coming of a person known as "the Christ," Maitreya, or Jesus.

Unfortunately, their efforts will simply bring us to the point where the Antichrist, not Jesus Christ, will step up onto the world's stage and rule humanity as the final human king. This is first revealed in the book of Daniel. The Antichrist will oversee what many Bible scholars refer to as the *Revised Roman Empire.*

Because of their common ideology, these groups may actually wind up working together toward their shared goal. It's easy to see NAR welcoming anyone from the New Age into their midst because the true Gospel is rarely if ever, preached with clarity. It's all about signs, wonders, and manifestations of God. Any seeker can join in.

So, we are getting to a point where we may see more cooperation between these three groups, but what about now? What is happening throughout the world that may be laying the groundwork for what's coming?

Since the election of President Donald Trump, those who hate him, led by the media, left-wing politicians, and celebrities, as well as many others throughout the world, have unleashed unprecedented and continuous attacks on him and his family. They have done everything possible to ruin or nullify his presidency. Despite this, Trump has made some great gains for America and for its people.

Unfortunately, President Trump has been surrounded by Dominionists and NAR apostles and prophets from the beginning. When we see a photo of Trump in the Oval Office encircled by people laying their hands on him and bowing in prayer, we understand that these individuals are largely Dominionists, proponents of NAR, or Kingdom Now ideology. What this means is that their basic intent is to not only improve the situation in America but to fully subdue the powers and principalities in the spiritual realm in order to bring about a massive change in the world so that Jesus can return. This belief in spiritual warfare runs rampant within NAR and

Kingdom Now. These people believe that as we take on the powers of darkness directly, and subdue them in the power of Christ, victories are gained, ground is recovered, and the battle is being won.

Interestingly enough, most who are seriously involved in the New Age believe the same type of thing but use different terminology. Instead of the power of Christ and prayer, they believe in the power of the "Christ consciousness" and the power of "positive energy." It's an important distinction in many ways, yet it's simply two sides of the same coin where New Age and NAR are concerned.

Another thing that both groups speak of is the travail that will occur prior to the peace that is coming to this earth. But biblical Christianity also speaks of the fact that the worst time on earth will yet occur in the future, called The Tribulation *(Matthew 24),* which is brought to an end by the physical return of Jesus and begins 1,000 years of actual peace throughout the world because of His rule.

Dominionists, NAR, and Kingdom Now followers all believe that people within Christendom must work to subdue the world for Jesus and that it involves a great deal of effort on our part. This effort will include many manifestations of God empowering those who come to Him for the purpose of fighting the enemy of our souls in the spiritual realm. It's really an absolutely absurd belief when all is said and done. Prayer is certainly powerful, but only as it is used to align our thinking, desires, and will with God's.

What about spiritual warfare as described by these groups? In Daniel 10, we learn that there was spiritual activity in the spiritual realm that kept one of God's angels from reaching Daniel quickly *(see also Job 1).* Daniel was experiencing great anxiety as a result of a vision that he had recently received from God, so much so that he mourned for three weeks *(Daniel 10:2)*! An angel was sent to provide greater clarity.

At the end of those three weeks, the angel arrived and gave Daniel more insight, specifically regarding what would happen to Daniel's "people" (the Jews of Israel), in the latter days *(Daniel 10:14).* The reason it took the angel three weeks to arrive is because he had been held back from arriving by the Prince of Persia, another powerful spirit in the heavenly realm, undoubtedly working for Satan to thwart God's plans.

During the three weeks of mourning, Daniel had no clue what was happening in the spiritual realm, though he would later find out. He was not praying or "fighting" in the spiritual realm against God's enemies during those three weeks. Daniel was simply trusting the Lord and waiting on Him.

However, NAR and Kingdom Now people believe that it is the Christian's responsibility to take on the powers of darkness in the spiritual realms. This is supposedly done through prayer and by decreeing that people have authority in these movements (apostles/prophets). The result – they say – is that evil is vanquished and through us, God gains the victory in that part of the spiritual realm. It's really hubris on steroids. While God chooses to use people, He does not need our help to accomplish His purposes. He does what He does, according to His plans and purposes.

Regarding the New Age's aspect on this, here is how one New Age website describes it:

The Age of Aquarius is causing great turmoil in order to make room for the new values of love, brotherhood, unity and integrity. Everything with Piscean values is being exposed and taken down. This includes governments, corporations, individuals, and even personal relationships. Many call this a disaster, as the world appears to be falling apart, but is it?

The Aquarian Age points to the direction of our own evolution in consciousness. We are each being asked to make a choice. We can cling to the old outdated values or adopt the new evolving ones. Our happiness and peace depends on our choice and the change will take place whether we like it or not.[26]

Notice the first paragraph especially. Because of the shift that they say is occurring, there will be great upheaval. They note it will extend to government, corporations, and relationships.

What has happened in the world since the election of Donald Trump? People in government are being exposed as corrupt politicians. Satan is literally divided against himself!

We've also seen one powerful individual after another being taken down by charges of sexual misconduct and harassment. Some came as no surprise, while others were a big surprise. There certainly appears to be massive upheaval throughout the world with many governments on the verge of collapse and social ills in many countries on the rise. New Agers tell us that this is all normal as one age segues into the next.

All of this travail and upheaval is seen as perfectly normal by the New Age, something that must occur, just like "birth pangs." Those within NAR tend to see many of these things (especially the constant firestorm surrounding Donald Trump) as the normal process that occurs when Satan

---

[26] https://www.3ho.org/3ho-lifestyle/aquarian-age/aquarian-shift-what-will-be-different (03/14/2018)

and his minions oppose those who work against them. Don't forget, numerous "prophets" in NAR predicted Trump's election. Satan had guessed ahead of time that Trump would be elected.

What many Christians fail to realize is how much Satan has counterfeited things that are found in Scripture. Jesus spoke of the "beginning of birth pangs" in His Olivet Discourse and the New Age speaks of a great upheaval prior to the "birth" of the new age *(Matthew 24, Mark 13, Luke 21).* This is what they believe is the coming Age of Aquarius.

In another example, Paul taught about the Rapture of the invisible Church, which would remove Christians from the earth sometime prior to the coming Great Tribulation. The New Age teaches that there is coming a rapture-like event that will remove millions from the earth and put them on another planet where they can evolve spiritually at their own pace.

Teachings like the ones above have been around within the New Age for decades since the 1940s at least. It is interesting to learn that many Christians don't understand what Satan has taught his followers within the New Age movement. We need to be aware that Satan has been extremely busy counterfeiting what the Bible actually teaches. If something is taught in Scripture, like the physical return of Jesus, doesn't it stand to reason that Satan is going to attempt to counterfeit that teaching within groups like the New Age so that when Satan's spiritual son is revealed, the world will receive him?

If Jesus is going to return physically (and He is), Satan clearly would want to prepare humanity for that major event. Rather than deny it (even though there are many who do deny it, even within Christendom), he will do all he can to prepare the world for it. However, he'll make the Antichrist, who will appear on the scene first, be mistaken for Jesus.

Because the Rapture is going to happen, obviously Satan needs to come up with a lie so that there will be a plausible explanation for those left behind. There must be a legitimate reason for all the missing people and the absolute catastrophe in its wake. These events will bring the world together in unity of purpose. It's quite clear from reading New Age materials that Satan has already laid the groundwork for how the explanation of the Rapture.

Other articles included have addressed this issue, but it is interesting to note that New Age author Barbara Marciniak *(Bringers of the Dawn)* wrote about the coming "Great Evacuation." In that future scenario, she says upwards of twenty million people will be removed from this planet to waiting spaceships. These ships will then transport those people to other planets where they can grow or "evolve" spiritually at their own pace without holding the rest of humanity back. The people removed are the "malcontents" who keep the planet from evolving to its next spiritual plane.

After this "evacuation" of over twenty million plus people, Marciniak notes that "*there will be a tremendous shift in consciousness for those who are remaining.*"[27] The new Age of Aquarius supposedly enters because of this shift. Paul says the "restrainer" will be taken out of the way which will give lawlessness free reign *(2 Thessalonians 2).*

A group known as The Ashtar Command says much the same thing and you can read about that in an article penned several years ago on my blog, "What Might Bring the World to Chaos?"[28] Documents from The Ashtar Command appeared in the very early 1950s and were originally provided by author George Van Tassel. As part of New Age beliefs, Satan has covered his bases fairly well. In the meantime, Christians argue about the Rapture, whether or not it will happen, and when it will happen. It doesn't matter when. The amount of counterfeit biblical teaching within the New Age should tell us that Satan knows without reservation that the Rapture will happen just as he knows Jesus will physically return to this earth one day.

New Age, Dominionism, NAR, and Kingdom Now all share a connection, which may allow them to work together in the future. They all twist the truth of Scripture to their own end. If you are a part of these movements, I cannot encourage you enough to remove yourself.

We will now discuss the influences that created the emphasis on the mystical within Christendom and then move onto another series designed to help us as Christians return to the study of God's infallible Word.

---

[27] https://studygrowknowblog.com/2017/02/20/what-might-bring-world-to-chaos/ (03/14/2018)

[28] Ibid

CHAPTER 7 NAR: Signs, Wonders, Bells & Whistles

Looking back on my involvement in the Charismatic Movement, I realize now that I was guilty of idolatry and motivated by self-centeredness. Unfortunately, I eventually realized that I was not chasing God at all. I was chasing the *experience* of what I believed to be God. There is a huge difference between the two.

I reasoned that God is supernatural and miraculous, therefore, to be in fellowship with Him, I must *experience* Him with signs and wonders and ecstatic experiences that are without rational or natural explanation. I was wrong. What is it that compels so many of us Christians to chase after an *experience* we believe is of God or from God?

While growing close to God in fellowship is certainly a scriptural endeavor and one that all Christians must pursue, it is literally *impossible* to discern whether any experience we might have is of God, Satan, or our own flesh.

Often, the way people determine validity is through the *subjectivity of feeling*. There is no other way to ascertain the truth. Galatians 5:22-26 clearly outlines the Fruit of the Spirit. Is *that* what people are getting from their pursuit of the ecstatic?

Look at the life Jesus lived. There were those who loved Him and many more who hated Him. There is nothing in Scripture that supports the pursuit of an ecstatic, experiential relationship that either the apostles or the average person enjoyed with Jesus. They related to Him as a human being because He was fully human.

Unlike the heretical teachings of people like Bill Johnson, pastor of Bethel Church in Redding, CA, and NAR apostle, who teaches that Jesus completely emptied Himself of His deity and lived life *only* as a human being fully dependent on the Holy Spirit;[29]Jesus remained *fully* God in the flesh, while also being fully human.

While Jesus "emptied" Himself of *something*, it was His own "self-will," not His deity. In other words, when He took on the form of humanity, He literally *clothed* Himself with that flesh, which hid His deity. He lived His

---

[29] http://pulpitandpen.org/2016/11/14/what-are-bill-johnsons-heresies/ (12/12/2017)

earthly life in constant submission in every way to the Father's will, moment-by-moment.

This does not mean that Jesus stopped being God while He lived on earth. It means He deliberately chose to do whatever the Father wanted Him to do and *only* used His power as God to complete what God the Father wanted from Him when miracles were needed.

Jesus' life became the perfect model for us as human beings regarding His consummate, daily submission to God the Father. In doing so, Jesus perfectly fulfilled every requirement of the Law without ever sinning, which made Him the perfect Person to offer Himself for *our* sin *(Revelation 5).*

Paul makes this "emptying" clear in his letter to the Philippians in chapter two. Though often misunderstood by many, Jesus did not empty Himself of His deity. He *covered* it with His humanity, yet His deity was very much still there, as evidenced by the transfiguration accounts *(Matthew 17:1–8, Mark 9:2–8, Luke 9:28–36).* In that instance, Jesus briefly allowed those around Him to see His natural glory as *God*, which was always resident within Him.

The normal day-to-day relationship Jesus had with those around Him does *not* provide a picture of one ecstatic experience after another, in spite of the fact that Jesus was and remains God. However, today we hear that miracles, signs, and wonders should be the *norm* for Christians, even though it was *not* the norm for those who followed Jesus on the earth during His days of ministry. Even *after* the Holy Spirit was poured out onto the people in the Upper Room, the miracles that resulted from that indwelling created the Church (Christ's Bride) by bringing 3,000 people to salvation that very day *(Acts 1-2).* The *wonder* created by the Presence of the Holy Spirit brought souls into the Church in true salvation.

The only "ecstatic" experience witnessed as a direct result of the outpouring of the Holy Spirit was the presence of "tongues." While this subject is hotly debated today, the truth is in that particular case; the believers were actually speaking in a *known* tongue (though unknown to them at the time). We know this because of the way people responded.

While some referred to them as being "drunk," it was not necessarily due to their *actions* or the way they walked. It was because it seemed to some that they were simply *babbling*, as a drunken person would do. The late Kenneth Hagin, a big name within the Signs and Wonders Movement, has stated that if people thought they were drunk, they must have been acting drunk, which would presume that they looked wobbly on their feet and spoke with slurred speech. *do you have a reference for this paraphrase?* That is not true *if* we consider the context of those verses.

Those visiting the area because of Pentecost were from all over the known Roman world. Many just happened upon this group of 120 believers who had just received the Holy Spirit. They heard them praising God and glorifying Him in their own native tongue. That amazed them, and why would it not?

When Peter preached, one of the first things he did was to discount the charge that they were drunk. He reminded them that it was early the morning, too early for drinking. He went on to fully explain to them the Gospel and reminded His listeners (most of whom were Jews and would have been familiar with the Scriptures) that what had happened was like what Joel had said in the Old Testament would occur at the end of this age.

Yes, throughout Acts, there were many miracles, signs, and wonders. However, it is interesting how many people in NAR or other signs and wonders groups take things out of context to support their own errant beliefs – that God exists to give us a miracle. They discount the truth of Scripture because of their mishandling of it.

The greatest miracle is being born again and having your name written in the Book of Life. Another wonderful miracle is the Holy Spirit's indwelling in the life of a believer as a seal of redemption *(Ephesians 1:13).* What does He produce? Galatians 5:22-26 spells it out for us.

But the fruit of the Spirit is love, joy, peace, forbearance, kindness, goodness, faithfulness, gentleness and self-control. Against such things there is no law. Those who belong to Christ Jesus have crucified the flesh with its passions and desires. Since we live by the Spirit, let us keep in step with the Spirit. Let us not become conceited, provoking and envying each other.

In Acts 5, we read an account of miracles that occurred through apostles.

Now many signs and wonders were regularly done among the people by the hands of the apostles. And they were all together in Solomon's Portico. None of the rest dared join them, but the people held them in high esteem. And more than ever believers were added to the Lord, multitudes of both men and women, so that they even carried out the sick into the streets and laid them on cots and mats, that as Peter came by at least his shadow might fall on some of them. The people also gathered from the towns around Jerusalem, bringing the sick and those afflicted with unclean spirits, and they were all healed. (Acts 5:12-16 ESV)

Notice it first says, "*many signs and wonders were regularly done.*" There is no mention of the unexplained ecstatic experiences that are prevalent in many Charismatic or NAR meetings. There is no mention of anyone being "slain in the Spirit," or even speaking in tongues here. To say that things were included is to read into the Scriptures. What very likely happened was what we read in the very last verse of the quoted Scripture above; people were healed and delivered from evil spirits *(v. 16).*

As a side note, the text says that people believed that Peter's shadow would heal them (a superstition tied to idol worship). Yet, the text does *not* say healings occurred because of it. The text *does* tell us that all were healed *after* they brought the sick to the apostles, not because of being near Peter's shadow.

Notice these signs and wonders were done by the "*hands of the apostles.*" God worked *through* the apostles to bring about healing to average people who were sick or possessed. God did this to *authenticate* their ministry, position, and authority in His Church. No one alive today has apostolic authority, no matter how many times they might claim it.

I cringe when I hear a speaker introduced as an "apostle" today, yet according to people in NAR, there are approximately 500 modern-day apostles alive right now. I have yet to read, however, of one legitimate claim of actual *healing* done by any of these so-called apostles. While it is one thing to claim an experience is by the power of the Holy Spirit, there is nothing we can turn to in Scripture that shows the Holy Spirit working the way He is claimed to be working today.

For instance, people will point to Paul's meeting with Jesus on the road to Damascus as an example of being "slain in the Spirit." This is false. Paul was simply walking along, and an exceedingly bright light shone down upon him. He likely lost his balance and fell to the ground. By the way, I have heard people say Paul was riding a horse and fell off the horse though the text makes no mention of a horse. This is a classic example of reading *into* the Scriptures.

Paul eventually relates his conversion story to the Jews in Jerusalem who was seeking his arrest, and again he simply says he "*fell to the ground*" *(Acts 22:6-11).* If you are walking along and trip, you might fall down to the ground. This may seem like a very small point, but it is often true that heresy starts with a very small point of error and grows from there.

Nevertheless, regarding signs and wonders, it seems clear enough that the miracles, signs, and wonders recorded in Scripture happened for a purpose. That main purpose was to bring God glory through the stamp of approval He Himself placed on the men He had called as apostles (or in very limited cases, those closest to them). People took notice.

Numerous sects and cults today are based on the false teaching that signs, wonders, and miracles are not only *available* for today's Christian, but should be *normal* day-to-day experiences. There is nothing in Scripture to support this.

The so-called signs and wonders today are nothing but Satan's attempts to provide a system that appears to imitate God. Because of that, Satan certainly has a growing audience. Again, I speak from my own experience as a past participant of the Charismatic Movement and their aberrant teachings as well as the things I witnessed and even participated in at times.

As recorded in Acts 2, the *invisible* Church was born with signs and wonders as recorded to call attention to the fact that it was *God's* work, not man's. However, the so-called ecstatic experiences that routinely occur within the arena of the Signs and Wonders Movement today are wholly inappropriate as a continuation of the reality of the invisible Church. These wonders were meant to establish the veracity of the invisible Church and God's work, in much the same way as the signs, wonders, and miracles performed by Jesus were evidence of His deity.

Today's "miracles" are said to accompany an alleged new work of God. We must ask what new work is God doing that He has not already revealed in Scripture? Today's signs and wonders cannot be supported through Scripture without a lot of twisting and reinterpreting. Even then, it is a stretch.

At one point during my participation in the Charismatic Movement, I began hearing a "voice" in my head that was absolutely *not* mine. At the time, I simply *assumed* it was God's voice because I had been praying to Him about something very specific. Unfortunately, I cannot prove one way or the other if that voice was God's voice. Because of that, I have no choice but to reject it thoroughly, though originally, I accepted it as being God's voice. It is important to note that at that time, I did not know my Bible well. I certainly did not test all things. Because of the fact that I was off the path theologically, I'm not sure any testing I might have done would have succeeded in solving the mystery.

What is telling, is the fact that during my involvement in the Charismatic Movement, no one stood up and suggested we test anything. This same thing applies to the Signs and Wonders Movement and specifically NAR today. No one seems interested in attempting to discern the *source* behind all these ecstatic experiences.

Why is this the case? It would seem that either people feel confident that the signs and wonders *are* from God or that they are too afraid to learn that they *are not* from God. If they learn the latter, they would be required to condemn the signs and wonders as being either of the flesh or of the devil. They do not want to do that because of the tremendously large "ministries" they would have to give up all well as the benefits they receive from those ministries. Remember, these people likely have no taxes taken out of their paychecks and anything associated with charitable organizations is free of taxation.

One individual named Phil presents his own testimony of being involved in the Signs and Wonders Movement and how he eventually left it. He has quite a bit to say about what he has learned.

Something supernatural is going on in the NAR movement. It just isn't emotional hype, although I believe heightened emotions are the gateway. I once thought this to be the Holy Spirit. I now believe it to be demonic, Satan disguising himself as an angel of light. I believe this to be none other than what the Bible calls the Spirit of the Antichrist. Whatever, you want to call it, its mission is to destroy the church from within, using a counterfeit light to accomplish it's [sic] purpose.[30]

Paul Gowdy, who bills himself as "a former Vineyard pastor," provides an additional testimony about being involved in what has been termed the Toronto Blessing and his ultimately leaving of the same. He explains what happened after his own church became involved in this "blessing."

After three years of being in the thick of the Toronto blessing our Vineyard assembly in Scarborough (East Toronto) just about self-destructed. We devoured one another, with gossip, backstabbing, division, sects criticism etc. After three years of 'soaking,' praying for people, shaking, rolling, laughing, roaring, ministering at TACF on their prayer team, leading worship at TACF, preaching at TACF, basically living at TACF we were the most carnal, immature and deceived Christians that I know. I remember saying to my friend and senior pastor at Scarborough Vineyard Church in 1997 that ever since the Toronto Blessing came we have just about fallen to bits! He agreed![31]

That is interesting, isn't it? I saw this happen not only in my life but in the lives of many others whom I came to know during my time in the Charismatic Movement. It seemed that the pursuit of God became substituted with the pursuit of things ecstatic. There was this constant push to pursue the "things of God," seen as signs, wonders, and miracles.

---

[30] https://bereanresearch.org/leaving-nar-church-phils-story/ (12/02/2017)
[31] https://truthforfree.com/html/article_torontopastorrepents.html (12/02/2017)

It should stand to reason that when people resort to living on experiences they believe to be from God, one of the tests is to note the *quality* of their lives *after* the experience. All too often, people involved take on the exact opposite demeanor that the Scriptures tell us to adopt. Why is that? It can only be due to one reason and that is the fact that these experiences are not of God. If these experiences are not of God, then these people are being drawn *away* from God.

Gowdy eventually left the Signs and Wonders Movement. He tried sharing his concerns with others in that movement but to no avail.

After one year into the blessing I spoke out at a pastors meeting and said 'guys we have shaken, rattled, rolled, laughed, cried, and bought the tee-shirt. But we have no revival, no salvation, no fruit and no increased evangelism so what's the deal?' I was soundly rebuked - who was I to expect to see fruit when the Lord was healing his broken people? We had been legalistic long enough and God was spending this time restoring his wounded and freeing us from legalism. I was told not to push the Lord and the harvest would come in his time.[32]

To introduce the next few chapters, let's look at the basic history of what has become today's New Apostolic Reformation (NAR). It is important to understand how aspects of Christendom have developed to the point we are now at, where deception is growing and sucking many into its demonic grasp.

It is interesting to note that each decade from the 1990s backward is noted for a specific movement, but all of them include some form of signs and wonders, which is simply Christian mysticism by another name.

In the mid-1800s, a philosophical outlook began to take root, which serves as the starting point on our timeline. From there, we will segue into the early 1900s with the Azusa Street Revival of 1906. Here is an outline of how the decades look[33].

- The New Order of the Latter Rain (NOLR) in the 1940s.
- The Voice of Healing Movement (VHM) in the 1950s.
- The Charismatic Renewal Movement (CRM) in the 1960s.
- The Shepherding/Discipleship Movement (SDM) in the 1970s.
- The Prophetic-Apostolic Movement (PAM) in the 1980s.

---

32 https://truthforfree.com/html/article_torontopastorrepents.html (12/02/2017)
33 https://churchwatchcentral.com/2017/05/06/resource-what-is-the-nar/ (12/02/2017)

- The New Apostolic Reformation (NAR) in the 1990s.

CHAPTER 8 New Order of the Latter Rain

It would not be an overstatement to say that this world is headed toward a one-world government. We have written about that in many books and articles, showing from Scripture how this will occur. Taking Scripture literally, in its most plain and ordinary sense, brings us to that unavoidable conclusion. It will be the fulfillment of the final kingdom first revealed in Daniel 2.

So how will this world get to that point? What will be the main means of transitioning the world to this coming one-world government, supported by a one-world religious system? Of course, in order to be viable, it must incorporate all the main aspects of global society, including religious expression.

Constance Cumbey breaks all of this down in her books and on her website.[34] As one might expect, it is not going to happen overnight, and it is extremely involved. This means that Satan has been working on this for many generations and his efforts seem to be picking up speed.

History keeps a record of how things have developed giving birth to religious movements that today appear to be segueing into the New Age Movement. These movements have the appearance of *Christianity*, and because of that, they deceive many.

By far, the most well-known religious movement today is called New Apostolic Reformation (NAR), as we have already introduced. It continues to captivate and draw away many within Christendom. Many who would never darken the door of a church are enamored with the "signs and wonders" that are associated with NAR. There is no real statement of Scripture-affirming beliefs. Any and all are welcome to come with the beliefs they already possess. Beyond this, curiosity, for no other reason, tends to draw a crowd.

We attended a conservative Protestant church when we lived in Northern California. We remained there for some time, until they introduced *40 Days of Purpose* by Rick Warren.

Rick Warren was unfamiliar to me at the time. I tried to read the book, but it simply did not sit well with me. I noticed obvious red flags while many others seemed to appreciate and enjoy the book.

---

[34] Cumbey.blogspot.com (accessed 11/20/17)

Around this same time, our senior pastor went on a mission trip to Africa. When he returned, he shared about the trip from the pulpit. He told the congregation he had met and worked with a number of Roman Catholic priests and missionaries and had grown fond of them and their commitment to the Lord. After about a week with them, he felt that he had more in common with Catholicism than he had previously thought. That, he says, surprised him.

Not long after this, he began speaking about the spiritual disciplines highlighted by Rick Foster and several Roman Catholic mystics before him. In the meantime, because of my concerns about the Rick Warren book, I had written an email to the pastor addressing those concerns. I did not hear back from him, and he never mentioned it when he saw me in church, so I didn't push it.

However, because of the increasing emphasis on spiritual disciplines from the pulpit on Sunday mornings, I sent him another email indicating we were leaving the church, and again briefly outlined my concerns. He responded almost immediately this time with something along the lines of, "*Well, God bless you in your future endeavors.*" I thought that was interesting until I learned that Rick Warren believed and taught that those in the congregation who could not accept new policies and "get with the program" should be encouraged to find another church and even asked to do so if necessary.

I later heard that the senior pastor eventually moved onto another much larger church in the Bay Area of California, one that was heavily into *spiritual formation*[35] (made up of the spiritual disciplines). But where did all of this originate? How did it find its way into the modern evangelical, Protestant church? As most things happen, it started small and became a *movement.* Over time, the name of the movement changed, but generally, the theological basis of the movement is essentially the same.

New Order of the Latter Rain (NOLR) The movement began in Canada in the 1940s and came about due to schisms within Pentecostalism.

The New Order of the Latter Rain was an organizational schism before it was a spiritual cause. Its key personnel emerged as the outcome of a succession of disputes involving faculty personnel of Bethel Bible Institute of Saskatoon, Canada, and the sponsoring Saskatchewan District of the Pentecostal Assemblies of Canada (the P.A.O.C). At the outset, there were charges and countercharges within the Institute between administration and

[35] https://www.gotquestions.org/spiritual-formation.html (12/02/2017)

faculty. But as the months passed, the Institute personnel were reconciled and the conflict came to be between the Institute and the District.[36]

By late 1947, though there was reconciliation, those who were discontent with the way things were resigned their positions at the institute and moved about 80 miles north. Three specific men who left were key players in the subsequent creation of something new: Rev. George Hawtin, Rev. Ernest Hawtin, and Rev. Percy Hunt. Once they landed in their new location (North Battleford), they joined with Rev. Herrick Holt, a pastor of the Four Square Church there. The four eventually founded and created "*Sharon Children's Homes and Schools which included a high school, an orphanage, a technical institute, and a Bible school.*"[37]

When school began again in the fall, many of the students who had previously attended Bethel Bible Institute ended up going north to attend Sharon. These students, along with the men who had left Bethel earlier, formed the nucleus of what became the *New Order of Latter Rain* (NOLR).

There were a few things that were the direct cause of the birth of the NOLR.

...a young woman at the [Sharon] Bible school prophesied that a great revival was about to come. Ernest Hawtin tells that the very next day, it did just that as the Holy Spirit fell with great power. It was called 'The Last Great Outpouring that was to consummate God's Plans on this Earth.'

There are always prophetic voices claiming that God is about to send a new "wave" of revival. It happened often during my days in the Charismatic Movement. The actual revivals never happened and even when meetings were held where signs and wonders occurred, there was no permanent growth for anyone. They created a good deal of excitement, a lot of hype, and much expended energy. In the end, there is simply a feeling of loss that pushes people to the next "revival."[38]

Apparently, Franklin Hall's book, *Atomic Power with God Through Fasting and Prayer* also played a part in setting the scene. The method of fasting described in it was done by students and staff.

Hall believed the Church was hindered in power and answered prayer, he claimed that even the prayers of pagans would be answered if they fasted. His solution, by fasting for long periods, Christians can receive a powerful anointing that would be that they would never be sick and would lead certain "overcomers" to holiness by stages of spiritual transformation

---

36 http://www.spiritwatch.org/firelatter2.htm (12/02/2017)
37 http://www.spiritwatch.org/firelatter2.htm (12/02/2017)
38 http://letusreason.org/Latrain7.htm (12/02/2017)

who would attain sinless perfection and immortality. That an immortal substance from Christ would come upon their bodies, a golden substance visible to all...that would glorify them and people would see and feel the fire of the Holy Spirit.

He taught a BODY-FELT salvation - the fire of God, the glory, had to be applied to the body for thirty days and would purge out all sickness, tiredness and weakness of the flesh and bring them to immortalization. These Perfected believers would experience power over the forces of gravity, they could teleport to wherever they wished. And there were practical benefits to this spiritual state where their clothes would not wear out, they would have no body odour (sic), so they would never need to wash.[39]

This is undoubtedly why at certain NAR meetings today, a type of gold dust[40] has been seen floating down from the rafters.

The special spiritual move that became the basis of the New Order movement began on February 11, 1948, some months after Sharon began operations. This day had been preceded by considerable emphasis and observance of long fasts as a means of special power with God. In extended chapel services for four days from February 11 through the 14th, the procedure emerged of calling out members of the audience and imparting a spiritual gift to them by the laying on of hands accompanied by a suitable prophecy. The authorization and direction of these activities was a series of vocal prophetic utterances by both students and their teachers.[41]

Interestingly enough, the emphasis on spiritual disciplines (fasting, enthusiastic sustained worship, etc.), is a means of drawing closer to God. This takes one down the road to mysticism as many New Age and ancient religious sects and cults emphasize these things. They are not prioritized within Christianity, although Christians are free to fast, to pray, and to focus their attention on God specifically at times. It should never be done as a ritual to "move" God in some way.

Chapel services featuring the impartation of gifts by the laying on of hands with prophecy took precedence over all other campus activities. Other worship patterns emerged that were somewhat unique in their time, with stress upon the visible manifestation of the charismata, and

---

39 http://letusreason.org/Latrain7.htm (12/20/2017)

40 https://absenceofchrist.wordpress.com/2015/08/15/gold-dust-miracle-at-a-global-awakening-meeting/ (12/20/2017)

41 http://www.spiritwatch.org/firelatter2.htm (12/20/2017)

such novelties as the so-called "heavenly choir." Before long, large numbers of visitors were attracted. Ultimately, all efforts to operate all educational institutions were suspended, and the North Battleford campus became simply a conference and camp meeting center...[42]

NOLR was known for signs and wonders. The movement emphasized these things from the start, and though the explanation of them has been modified over the decades, the same basic premises undergird the movement of today, which has ultimately morphed into NAR.

Within the movement, the gift of prophecy was just as important then as it is now. It was believed that by the laying on of hands, people would receive this particular gift as led by the Spirit. This is called *impartation* and followers viewed prophetic utterances as equal with Scripture. Note the following quote below with my emphasis added.

In New Order practice, the gift of prophecy was made to function routinely to identify individuals by name. It would then proceed to instruct its subjects in a detailed manner regarding personal and practical affairs, both in regard to the work of God, and in matters of everyday living. Such prophecies were considered to be **certain, unalterable, and above evaluative scrutiny**.[43]

With respect to the practice of "imparting" gifts of prophecy or other things to people, the group's leadership denied that *people* were imparting anything. In fact, Rev. R. E. McAlister wrote a pamphlet about it, and he "*is believed to be the first Canadian to have received the baptism in the Spirit at Azusa in 1906,*"[44] nearly four decades before this.

McAlister's "'*The Manifestation of the Spirit' argued that gifts are resident in the triune God, and neither received, imparted, nor confirmed in humans, but manifested.*"[45] It is interesting to watch videos from NAR, Word of Faith, and Charismatic services where signs and wonders occur. Quite often, we are led to believe that these modern-day apostles and prophets leading these services have the power actually to impart or heal. Kenneth Hagin taught that the anointing [of the Holy Spirit] is transferable to other people simply by the laying on of hands. Of course, Hagin also taught the person has to be receptive to that anointing or will not receive it.

All of what we call New Order of Latter Rain has its roots in the Azusa Street Revival. It occurred in Los Angeles, California, in 1906 and lasted

---

42 Ibid

43 http://www.spiritwatch.org/firelatter2.htm (12/20/2017)

44 http://www.spiritwatch.org/firelatter2.htm (12/20/2017)

45 Ibid

until about 1915. It is considered to be the origin of the Pentecostal movement, and it began under African-American preacher, William J. Seymour. Services held during the revival evidenced speaking in tongues and alleged healings. It was panned then not only by Christian theologians but by the media as well.

Among first-hand accounts were reports of the blind having their sight restored, diseases being cured instantly, and immigrants speaking in German, Yiddish, and Spanish, all the while being spoken to in their native language by uneducated black members who translated the languages into English by "supernatural ability."[46]

The Los Angeles Times reported on one of the meetings by stating, "*Breathing strange utterances and mouthing a creed which it would seem no sane mortal could understand...the newest religious sect has started in Los Angeles.*"[47]

Another Los Angeles paper related the following, "*...disgraceful intermingling of the races...they cry and make howling noises all day and into the night. They run, jump, shake all over, shout to the top of their voice, spin around in circles, fall out on the sawdust blanketed floor jerking, kicking and rolling all over it. Some of them pass out and do not move for hours as though they were dead. These people appear to be mad, mentally deranged or under a spell. They claim to be filled with the spirit. They have a one eyed, illiterate Negro as their preacher who stays on his knees much of the time with his head hidden between the wooden milk crates. He doesn't talk very much but at times he can be heard shouting, 'Repent,' and he's supposed to be running the thing... They repeatedly sing the same song, 'The Comforter Has Come.*"[48]

Azusa birthed Pentecostalism (and interestingly enough, the NOLR movement that indirectly stemmed from it) was actually renounced by Assemblies of God in 1949, but that didn't stop the movement.

NOLR has continued to grow because there are always people who want "more" of God. The problem is, they want it *quickly*, through mystical and ecstatic experiences rather than the longer tried and true way of reading God's Word daily to gain a greater understanding of who God is and how He works.

---

[46] https://en.wikipedia.org/wiki/Azusa_Street_Revival (03/12/2018)

[47] Ibid

[48] https://en.wikipedia.org/wiki/Azusa_Street_Revival (03/12/2018)

What became of the New Order of Latter Rain? It continued and changed its name to *Voice of the Healing Movement*, which will be addressed next.

CHAPTER 9 Voice of Healing Movement of the 1950s

Today, the entire Signs and Wonders Movement, led by people who claim apostolic or prophetic authority, can be summed up with Paul's words to the Corinthian believers.

For such men are false apostles, deceitful workmen, disguising themselves as apostles of Christ. (II Corinthians 11:13 ESV)

The leaders of the New Apostolic Movement today and those who have come before them are all "*false apostles, deceitful workmen, disguising themselves as apostles of Christ.*" Though they may ultimately believe their own disguise, they are no less culpable or responsible for causing people to fall away from truth to embrace the lies they peddle, often for their own self-aggrandizement and enrichment. Of course, Paul points out that Satan is an *angel of light*, so naturally, his human servants use disguises to hide the truth about themselves (II Corinthians 11:14).

The main name associated with the Voice of Healing Movement (VOHM) is William Branham. It is claimed by many that he is the greatest prophetic voice of the 20th century.

Branham was a minister within Pentecostalism where a variety of signs and wonders encircled him wherever he preached. In fact, Branham was known for his "pillar of fire" that would at times rest on his shoulder, or move around the crowd to which he ministered. Branham put great stock in his "angel" whom he said was always with him. Please note that he stated an *angel* worked in and through him, not *God* Himself.[49]

It is unfortunate that within the prophetic Signs and Wonders Movement there is so much doctrinal error persisting today. What is even more tragic is the fact that these errors are routinely accepted as truth by so many. This is due to one fact and one fact only: the teachings that are presented often come with some manifestations of signs and wonders. Instead of using the Bible to corroborate or discount whatever is being *taught* to them, people willingly accept the teachings as from God based solely on the presence of signs and wonders. How easy is Satan's job where too many seekers are concerned?

---

[49] http://letusreason.org/Latrain9.htm (12/20/2017)

As we read the Bible, we learn that Satan is a very powerful, supernatural being. His intellect alone far exceeds that of the smartest human. He exists in the spiritual realm, unseen by human eyes, though he can *affect* what occurs in this realm *(Job 1).* He does what normal human beings cannot do, and he has the advantageous cloak of invisibility that works in his favor.

When Satan masquerades as an *angel of light*, he does so for only two purposes. First, Satan attempts to imitate God *(Isaiah 14).* Second, Satan spiritually deceives people *(II Corinthians 11:14).*

C. S. Lewis has said, Satan's greatest trick is making people think he does not exist (my paraphrase). For the Christian, Satan's greatest trick is causing Christians to think his lies are actually truth from God. Sadly, it is exceedingly easy for Satan to do this since so many Christians are biblically illiterate. Is it any wonder that people such as Branham gain such a tremendous following and are revered to this day?

Branham started out in the Pentecostal Baptist church, a denomination that emphasizes the baptism of the Holy Spirit *after* conversion. This baptism is said to be evidenced by speaking in tongues. Branham later switched over to Oneness Pentecostalism (modalism), which is what T. D. Jakes also believes. Pastor Steven Furtick introduced Jakes to his congregations as one of the greatest preachers of this generation.

Oneness Pentecostalism or modalism[50] is the denial of the Trinity. Modalism is the belief that there is one God as only one Person, who is at times the Father, the Son, or the Holy Spirit. God will change identities as needed.

Because of that belief alone, Branham became heretical. His denial of a very essential part of God's character, the Trinity, should have expelled him from being a preacher, but like T. D. Jakes, people loved Branham. Just because human beings have no capacity to appreciate or understand the exact nature of the Trinity fully does not provide a good enough reason to deny it any more than the person who cannot believe in God chooses atheism in denying God's existence.

Throughout his whole life, Branham, unfortunately, seemed to be the recipient of supernatural occurrences. He claimed that at his birth he saw a light come down upon him. In another instance, at the age of three, he allegedly heard a voice from a tree telling him where he would live, which he later said came true.

[50] https://www.gotquestions.org/Modalistic-Monarchianism.html (12/05/2017

These events could have all been embellishments of actual situations that occurred, had demonic origins, or been outright lies. On the other hand, he could have seriously believed they happened, but their occurrence does not prove that they were from God simply because they happened. If they *did* occur, it is far more likely that Satan or one of his angels was attempting to deceive Branham into hearing a particular voice that he would eventually come to believe was God.

God does not speak to us in this way today. There is no need for it. You should reject anything that presents itself in this fashion. Reject it and submit to God. Resist the devil, and he will flee from you *(James 4:7).* This does not mean that God won't "urge" us to move in one direction or another as part of the way He leads us. I'm talking about audible voices, dreams, and visions. Be very leery of these things.

Since we have the full canon of God's Word and the indwelling Holy Spirit's enablement,[51] we are not lacking any knowledge from God or about God. God leads us in ways that do not include voices. He acts upon and uses circumstances. He opens and closes doors. He does not turn His children into mind readers or clairvoyants, or people who "hear" voices. This is what Satan does to those he attempts to ensnare. This deception makes them feel powerful and spiritual.

Branham stated that he was commissioned by an angel in 1946 and shortly thereafter began his healing ministry which included revivals. Numerous photos were taken of Branham with a type of light or "fire" above his head or shoulder. Branham believed that these occurrences were God's stamp of approval on him and his ministry. He simply assumed these "signs" were from God.

The book of Acts includes many instances of signs and wonders that occur throughout the ministry of the apostles, with only a few exceptions. There are, however, no living apostles today. There are no prophets. There is no need for them.

NAR exists as an attempt to show that God has raised new, modern-day apostles and if they are truly apostles after the order of the original

---

[51] **CPH FOOTNOTE**: The Holy Spirit and Jesus (http://tiny.cc/sibwqy), The Holy Spirit and the Apostles (http://tiny.cc/vgbwqy), The Holy Spirit in the First Century and Today (http://tiny.cc/pabwqy), The Holy Spirit and the Apostolic Church (http://tiny.cc/3fbwqy), The Holy Spirit and the World (http://tiny.cc/ffbwqy), The Work of the Holy Spirit (http://tiny.cc/sjbwqy), How Are We to Understand the Indwelling of the Holy Spirit? (http://tiny.cc/1mbwqy), How Do We Receive the Holy Spirit Today? (http://tiny.cc/lel7qy), Are Answers to Our Prayerful Requests Absolutely Guaranteed? (http://tiny.cc/6yk7qy), Is Foreknowledge Compatible with Free Will? (http://tiny.cc/1i1isy)

apostles, it is argued they have the same authority as the original twelve. It is also stated that we should expect to see "signs and wonders" wherever these "apostles" minister. Since we *do* see signs and wonders, we should also believe and follow them, because it is assumed that the signs and wonders are from God. Unfortunately, this circular reasoning is accepted by many followers of NAR.

There are many individuals within the current NAR movement that are seen and accepted as today's apostles. Todd Bentley, Che Ahn, Bill Johnson, Randy Clark, Heidi Baker, the late C. Peter Wagner, and others, are all said to be part of today's new apostles and prophets. They truly believe they have the same authority given to the original apostles. Through reciprocal self-aggrandizing, they expect average Christians to believe them and accept what they say as equal to the Bible without question.

The following is part of a conversation between Todd Bentley and Che Ahn that references William Branham, from *Church Watch Central.*

Che Ahn: And there's a 'Branham' anointing on you. There's a double portion of it. The Lord is raising you up. I felt like I want to say that you must decrease, you must increase. And I say that for all the Revivalists, I say that with all my friends.[52]

As Kenneth Hagin taught, an anointing is "transferable." Someone who has it can pass it along to others who do not. This is the main reason for the "laying on of hands" at these NAR-related events and services. Even though Paul warned Timothy to be careful about whom he laid hands on, the leaders within NAR lay hands on their followers without restraint *(I Timothy 5:22).* It is a great way for Satan to pass along his curse from one unsuspecting individual to another. It opens the door to satanic oppression and possession.

In I Timothy, Paul was referring to the laying on of hands to *appoint*, not *anoint*, elders into leadership roles in the local church. Paul wanted Timothy to be very careful, and in a similar way, those asked to consider becoming elders were to take time to pray and consider the responsibility of the position before agreeing. For Paul, the laying on of hands was an official *ceremonial* act. Today, in Charismatic, Signs and Wonders Movements, and NAR circles, the laying on of hands imparts what they say is a "blessing" or "anointing." This idea has its roots in the Old Testament, but it was clearly not in vogue during Paul's day nor found in his teachings.

---

52 https://churchwatchcentral.com/2017/05/03/transcript-of-che-ahn-and-todd-bentley-confirming-heidi-baker-and-others-as-apostles-promoting-new-breed-heresy/ (12/05/2017

There were numerous instances where Jesus healed without ever touching anyone and at least one instance where someone deliberately touched Jesus and received healing *(Luke 8:43-48).* The laying on of hands was not mandatory or required. Today, the meaning of it has completely changed from its original biblical meaning and purpose.

Notice in the above conversation between Che Ahn and Bentley that Ahn says Bentley has a "*double portion*" of Branham's anointing. This is often stated within NAR and Charismatic circles because it evokes the idea of true authority. Anyone who knows anything about the Bible will recall Elijah and Elisha (or Moses and Joshua). Elisha received a double portion of God's anointing when he saw Elijah depart from this earth and be taken up to into heaven *(II Kings 2).* However, both Elijah and Elisha were authentic prophets whom God had called. Todd Bentley? Che Ahn? William Branham? They have to *say* they are prophets because that is what creates the aura of authority and importance for them and for others within that movement.

Take note, also, that Che Ahn used the term "*Revivalists.*" This is code for "apostle," according to *Church Watch Central*, as practitioners believe the office of apostle and prophet is being *revived.* They publicly downplay the obvious fact that they believe there are apostles today who are said to hold the same position and authority as the original twelve.

Around 1955, Branham's ministry began to suffer financially. The IRS charged him with tax evasion. A great deal of money had come to the ministry, but it was revealed that there were people who were taking advantage of that situation, siphoning the funds. Branham, however, lived a life of poverty, not seeming to care about the money. Eventually, an out-of-court settlement was arranged.

Toward the end of his life, Branham's teachings became even more esoteric and seriously heretical. At one event, he even shared the pulpit with Jim Jones of the doomed cult, The People's Temple.

Branham died as a result of a car crash in 1965, and some of his followers believed he would rise from the dead. Kenneth Hagin said that God had told him two years prior that He was going to take Branham home early because of his heretical teachings. It is interesting that he never shared that with anyone until after Branham was dead. It is also interesting that Hagin was never concerned about his own heresy and is still lauded by many within NAR today.

Branham had come to believe, among other things, that hell was not eternal and that Eve had sexual relations with Satan, giving birth to Cain (Serpent's Seed doctrine). He clearly arrived at these conclusions based on something extra-biblical, not based on God's Word. These, along with his other non-biblical beliefs he stated were given to him by divine revelation, convinced him they were true.

Michael Moriarty in his book, *The New Charismatics* states:

Branham's aberrational teachings not only cultivated cultic fringe movements like the Latter Rain Movement and the Manifested Sons of God, but they also paved a pathway leading to false predictions, revelatory madness, doctrinal heresies, and a cultic following that treated his sermons as oral Scriptures.[53]

Let's take a look at the next phase of the movement in our next chapter.

---

53 https://en.wikipedia.org/wiki/William_M._Branham (12/05/2017)

CHAPTER 10 Charismatic Renewal Movement

The reliance on special signs from God is the mark of an immature person; an individual that cannot simply believe the truth as presented, but must have a special, miraculous sign as the symbol of authority from God.[54]

The above comment illustrates one of the problems that exists in Christendom. Of course, those involved in movements that stress signs and wonders deny that they are seeking signs to believe in God as Jesus' contemporaries did. They would argue that they are simply seeking God, not signs. It is argued that because God is supernatural, His Presence (manifestation) would be seen in signs and wonders as *normative.*

We have highlighted the New Order of Latter Rain and the Voice of Healing Movement previously. These were representative of the 1940s and 1950s, and both movements included many signs and wonders. However, do all the signs and wonders in the world bring people into a closer walk with God? Are people walking more in *obedience* to His commands, to live for Him daily because of these signs and wonders?

Signs and wonders are certainly more exciting, aren't they? Since they appear to be of supernatural origin, it is often accepted that they must be of God. When all is said and done, what remains? Have people truly and permanently *changed* for the better? Are Christians following Jesus in greater humility and obedience?

Many of the leaders in these movements often seem very carnal. It is not uncommon for them to be immersed in scandal. They often point to numbers though in an attempt to prove their credibility and integrity.

Todd Bentley states on his Fresh Fire website, "*We have seen over a million people in 65 nations make a decision for Christ in our crusades, having heard the Gospel preached, and seeing and experiencing the Word heal, save, set free, and deliver in signs, wonders, and miracles.*"[55]

The problem with this is that when Bentley's revival services are viewed, a clear presentation of the Gospel is normally completely *absent.* What *is* prevalent are signs and wonders that are simply accepted as being

---

[54] Finding the Will of God, Dr. Bruce Waltke, p 32
[55] http://www.freshfireusa.com/vision (12/05/2017)

from God. The rationale is that the signs and wonders are a manifestation of God moving through the crowd. It is then assumed that as people in the crowd are "slain in the spirit," speak in tongues, scream in agony, and shake like an exercise machine, God has "overshadowed" them with His Presence. This is then taken to mean that the person has "made a decision for Christ."

Is this the testimony of Scripture? In Acts 2, the very day of the birth of the Church, Peter preached a very clear message about the sacrifice of Jesus and what it means. For everyone who comes to Him in faith believing that what He accomplished on Calvary's cross brings salvation to the penitent person will be saved. In Romans 10:10-11, Paul clearly and succinctly presents the Gospel message. In fact, throughout the New Testament we see this message repeated over and over. It is very hard to miss.

Yet, we do *not* hear this message presented at these gatherings led by heretics like Todd Bentley, Bill Johnson, Rick Joyner, Heidi Baker, and others. It is at its core, a gathering of people who seek signs as evidence of the manifestation and work of God. God is expected to *perform* for them, to *prove* that He exists and that He is there. I cannot help but wonder how many of these individuals will learn that they never knew Jesus at all upon their death *(Matthew 7:21-23).* I hope that some actually know Jesus, and have only seriously (temporarily) gotten off path. The alternative causes one to shudder.

Though a struggle, the Christian life is fairly mundane. By this I mean that, in order to get to know God, one must first commit him/herself to *wanting* to know Him in a living, vibrant relationship. This occurs at salvation and is an ongoing commitment, much like a marriage vow. It is to be taken seriously and lived out daily. This is called *sanctification* and is a very real *process.*

Two married people are not supposed to avoid adultery one day only to give into it the next. The marriage vow is to be taken seriously with each partner recognizing the reality of that covenant on a daily basis for as long as they both shall live. Those vows should prompt them to not tempt themselves by allowing situations to occur where their marriage vows can be compromised. Those two people should grow in love and commitment to one another with each passing day. Without a concrete commitment to one another, it might be easy for two people to grow apart.

It is the same in our relationship with God in Christ. As Christians, we are to take very seriously our commitment to Him. We are to live in a way that fulfills the "law of Christ" that Paul often refers to throughout his writings. This is summed up in Christ's words to "love God with all of our heart, mind, and soul and to love others as we love ourselves" *(Mark 12:30-*

31). What *aids* us there? Is it signs and wonders, or is it the indwelling Holy Spirit who empowers us, convicts of sin, and helps us move on to maturity in Christ?

Is living the Christian life something that we grow into as we mature in Christ or is it something that happens instantaneously through the presence of signs and wonders? Good marriages do not happen overnight. Great effort goes into making them solid and healthy. So it is with our relationship with God in Christ. It takes time, dedication, commitment, and effort – *not* to save us, but for us to *grow* in Christ *after* we have gained salvation.

The Charismatic Movement is still around today. While the emphasis is on specific signs and wonders, the name has changed. These movements are now interconnected with new incarnations. This gives the impression that God is truly doing something "new," when in reality, there is nothing new at all. It is simply introduced as new by leaders of that movement because of a different emphasis.

Anyone who steps foot inside the Charismatic Movement and stays a while understands its origins in America. The name of the one main individual through whom the movement started and grew is common knowledge, but for the sake of those who are unaware, here are the basics.

On April 3, 1960, the Charismatic Movement went public when Father Dennis Bennett, an Episcopal priest announced to his Van Nuys, CA, congregation that he had personally spoken in tongues and that he believed that this was the pattern for the church. Later in 1966 the Charismatic Movement penetrated the Roman Catholic Church where it was readily received by a laity and clergy opened, via Vatican II, to new ideas on church renewal.[56]

Dennis Bennett is considered to be the man through which the modern-day Charismatic Movement (Renewal) occurred in America, the latest version of today's NAR. Bennett said he spoke in tongues, and of course, tongues for the Charismatic means speaking in an unknown "heavenly" language, a language that only God understands. Even though the person praying the unknown language doesn't understand what they're saying, they believe they are "blessed" because of it. You may even recall one of his most well-known books, *Nine O' Clock In The Morning.*

---

56 http://www.christianfallacies.com/articles/forsyth/historyOfCharismaticMovement.html (12/05/2017)

Paul has a great deal to say about tongues and even if we agree that Paul was speaking about tongues as an *unknown* heavenly language (we don't believe he was), he certainly downplayed that particular gift with the Corinthian believers. Yet, this is essentially the sign/wonder that began the modern-day Charismatic Movement in America.

When I was involved in the Charismatic Movement, speaking in tongues was always seen as a heavenly blessing and those who practiced the gift were obviously more "spiritual" than those who did not have it. This was the implication. This was also the problem with Corinthian believers who thought that the "tongues" gift made people super-Christians. They even cast aspersions and doubt where Paul was concerned, which is why he stated that he was glad he spoke in tongues more than any of them *(I Corinthians 14:18, chapters 12 – 14 specifically).* They were implying that they were more spiritual than the apostle Paul because of their constant use of tongues.

For Paul, tongues - speaking in real languages not known to the speaker - was not high on the list of gifts from God. For the Corinthians, it most certainly was, and that opinion is shared with the Charismatic Movement. Speaking in tongues is allegedly evidence of the "second blessing," the baptism of the Holy Spirit. Those who don't have that ability, then, have not been baptized by the Holy Spirit.

I recall many authors and leaders within the movement whom all pushed this doctrine. Jamie Buckingham, Harold Hill, Joyce Landorf, Bob Mumford, and many others were all looked up to as though they had the very words of God. Sadly, as often happens in these movements, religious leaders are followed, and their books are read as though they are imprinted with the very words of God, to the extent that the Bible, God's actual Word to us, takes a back seat. I voraciously read many of these books, but not God's Word. I currently have a few remaining in my library as reference only.

The Charismatic Movement is also sometimes known as the "second wave" of the Holy Spirit, with the first wave going back to the Azusa Street Revival of 1906, which gave birth to Pentecostalism. To this day, the Charismatic Movement is popular in segments of the Roman Catholic Church as well, and it is for this reason that people from various non-Roman Catholic denominations are drawn together with Roman Catholics to worship.

In these ecumenical settings, serious theological differences are set aside as all seek to "know" God, normally through signs and wonders. The tragedy is that due to many of the pagan origins of Roman Catholicism, it resembles the Corinthians continuing to celebrate idolatrous meals inside cultic temples, thinking there was nothing wrong with their acts *(I Corinthians 10).* They believed that since they were now Christians and not under the Law, they didn't have to worry about where they ate or the particular meats that they consumed (even if they *had* been sacrificed to idols). Paul explained that to avoid the appearance of evil, they should stop participating in these idolatrous celebrations. It should also be done for "conscience" sake; not theirs, but for those who had not yet come to faith and continued to worship idols.

Unfortunately, it is essentially the same thing when worshipping with Roman Catholics. Theirs is a works-based, ritualistic religion that preaches salvation by works, *plus* faith, *plus* the traditions of the church. To worship with Roman Catholics in their churches means to agree with their teachings. Attending a Roman Catholic funeral as a show of respect for someone we know who has died is at times appropriate. However, worshipping with someone in their setting, whose beliefs are diametrically opposed to Scripture, is to be avoided because it sends the wrong message to *them.*

The Charismatic Movement itself began to wane in the late 1970s. The leaders within the movement "*Oral Roberts, Larry Lea, Earl Paulk, Dick Iverson, Kenneth Copeland, Kenneth Hagin, Bob Tilton, etc., [proclaimed] that the 'charismatic movement' is over and God's 'new move' is underway.*"[57] According to them, God is always doing something new, but that is not the message of Scripture.

In all of these movements, the emphasis is always put on people's *feelings.* Feelings determine truth. All of this is simply a principle of Cultural Marxism (emotional virtue, a.k.a., political correctness). Society has learned to determine truth emotionally, rather than by discerning the truth of God's Word. People like to be their own judge. They don't want to have to rely on God's truth. Certainly, we see that among the heathen of the world, but for too long we've been seeing it among those who claim to follow Jesus as well. The Bible promises it will only worsen as the end of this age approaches. Spare yourself the problems associated with these unscriptural movements by refusing to allow yourself to be sucked into them ignorantly.

The Charismatic Movement gave way to the third wave of God moving among people and like its predecessors it has had a number of incarnations over the years. The common through lines are the *experiences* that are sought, and the seeming loss of control exhibited by those who receive those experiences. This will be discussed next.

---

[57] http://www.rapidnet.com/~jbeard/bdm/Psychology/chr/more/hist.htm (12/05/2017)

CHAPTER 11 Losing Control in the Name of God?

When viewing videos of the so-called worship services of New Apostolic Reformation (NAR), Word of Faith (WOF), or just about anything Charismatic, it quickly becomes clear that there is absolutely no order in those services. Proponents argue that what we are seeing is a move or manifestation of God, therefore to condemn or attempt to squelch it is to squelch the Holy Spirit. But is that truly the case?

If a revelation is made to another sitting there, let the first be silent. For you can all prophesy one by one, so that all may learn, and all be encouraged, and the spirits of prophets are subject to prophets. ***For God is not a God of confusion but of peace...*** *(I Corinthians 14:30-33a ESV)*

If anything be revealed to another that sitteth by, let the first hold his peace. For ye may all prophesy one by one, that all may learn, and all may be comforted. And the spirits of the prophets are subject to the prophets. ***For God is not the author of confusion, but of peace****, as in all churches of the saints. (I Corinthians 14:30-33a KJV)*

One sentence has been emphasized in each version of the Scripture to help us focus on the truth as revealed by a true apostle, Paul of Tarsus. The problems within the Corinthian church were manifold. They highly valued the sign gifts and specifically tongues, just like today's Charismatic Movement and its many branches. Unfortunately, there was great disorder and confusion in the Corinthian church because of it. Paul corrected their misconception numerous times by pointing out that speaking in tongues, in and of itself, was not the highly valued gift they were making it out to be. In fact, he said that other gifts were far more important *(I Corinthians 12).*

It would seem from reading Paul's first letter to the Corinthians that their church services were an absolute mess, causing Paul's frustration to rise to the surface on numerous instances throughout the letter. Some became drunk at the Lord's table, while others partook of nothing. Paul told them to eat at home *(I Corinthians 11:17-34).*

One can only imagine how much confusion existed at that church. Reading through the first letter to the Corinthians is like reading a description of the situation within Charismatic and signs/wonders gatherings. There is no decency amidst all the confusion. Proponents would likely argue that there is no confusion at all. I cannot imagine that Paul would agree.

Thus tongues are a sign not for believers but for unbelievers, while prophecy is a sign not for unbelievers but for believers. If, therefore, the whole church comes together and all speak in tongues, and outsiders or unbelievers enter, will they not say that you are out of your minds? (I Corinthians 14:22-23 ESV)

Paul's question in the last sentence is rhetorical, isn't it? Imagine an unsaved person walking into a Charismatic or NAR service where people are lying on the floor, laughing deliriously, speaking what sounds like gibberish, screaming in agony as if on fire, and dancing or twirling around in madness.

How does any of this bring *glory* to God? According to Paul, it doesn't, because an unsaved person seeing that would likely think, "*These people are lunatics!*"

Notice that Paul specifically states that "tongues" are a sign for unbelievers. How so? In Acts 2, just before Peter preached the sermon that brought 3,000 souls into the Church in one day, the 120 who had waited in the Upper Room were speaking in "tongues." Of course, their tongues were *actual* languages given to them by God, the Holy Spirit, who used that *sign* for unbelievers gathered in Jerusalem. While some denigrated the 120 disciples as being "drunk," many listeners heard them praising God in their own native tongue, which was not native to those speaking! That's the miracle! Tongues are a sign for those who are *not yet saved.*

Yet in Charismatic circles, tongues are constantly used in and out of church services where there is virtually no interpretation. In every service I ever attended during my involvement with the Charismatic Movement, English was spoken by everyone. In my experiences, there was not one instance of anyone interpreting a person who spoke in tongues. There was, according to Paul, no reason for tongues to be used at all.

If you attend a service where 300 hundred people are all speaking in tongues, and an unsaved person walks in, what will they receive from it? Charismatic circles completely ignore this question, to their shame. They continue to elevate the gift of "tongues," seeing it as a second blessing that tends to promote the speaker to an elevated status. Paul argued against this, yet it persists.

Paul also had some important things to say about *prophets* at the Corinthian church. It is understandable that prophets would have still existed during the first century because God was still revealing His Word.

This continued until the time was right for the entirety of the Bible to be compiled together in what we today call a closed canon of Scripture.

I have met people who put no stock in the "councils" that determined which books became part of what we now call the Bible. They say that *man* made those decisions. What they fail to understand is that they are actually criticizing *God* not man, by their statements. They are actually denying the ability of God to put the final touches on His revealed, written Word to humanity. However, they view themselves as "spiritual" because of their humanistic reasoning. They are not spiritual; they are arrogant. All their thinking really does is slap God in the face.

Biblical history is replete with example after example of how God used even ungodly and unsaved people to bring His will to fruition. This is biblical fact. Yet, we are to believe that somehow, mere men were able to keep God Almighty from bringing the final version of His Word together and presenting it as His final Word to humanity? What hubris to think that.

During the Corinthians' time, God was still revealing his secrets and mysteries; what has become our theology today. Paul acknowledges this, and he himself reveals numerous "mysteries" in his writings. It shouldn't be difficult for Christians today to understand that the first-century believers did not have all of God's Word. Prophets were still very much needed during Paul's day. Of course, there were plenty of false prophets as well, which he and others often wrote about.

How about now? Are prophets needed today? Should we really have to answer that question? Unfortunately, we do, because there are so many who claim to have the gift of prophecy today. These "false prophets," and those who follow them, believe God is still adding to His Word. There can be no other way of looking at it. Either God is still writing His Word through current "revelations" by those who claim the gift of prophecy or He is not. It cannot be both. If He *is*, then that means the things these modern-day prophets reveal today are *equal* in authority to what has been previously revealed as part of God's Word. If He is *not* continuing to reveal Himself in this way, then they have no authority.

Regarding the false prophets of his day, Paul made things very clear in I Corinthians 14:30-32, as highlighted above.

If a revelation is made to another sitting there, let the first be silent. For you can all prophesy one by one, so that all may learn and all be encouraged, ***and the spirits of prophets are subject to prophets.*** *For God is not a God of confusion but of peace. (ESV)*

Please notice the text in bold. It is very important and it is often missed. Paul says, "*...and the spirits of prophets are subject to prophets.*" What does that mean? Very simply, it means that God does *not* overtake the prophet so that the prophet loses control of himself. Dr. Thomas Constable, noted theologian and commentator explains.

Prophets were to control themselves when speaking ("the spirits of prophets are subject to prophets"), even when giving new revelation (cf. vv. 27-28). The nature of this gift was that it did not sweep the prophet into a mindless frenzy. Pagans, on the other hand, who received demonic revelations, frequently lost control of themselves. Inability to control oneself was no evidence that the prophet spoke from God. On the contrary, it indicated that he was not submitting to God's control, because "God" produces "peace," not "confusion."

The theological point is crucial: the character of one's deity is reflected in the character of one's worship. The Corinthians must therefore cease worship that reflects the pagan deities more than the God whom they have come to know through the Lord Jesus Christ (cf. 12:2-3). God is neither characterized by disorder nor the cause of it in the assembly.[58]

Again, the apostle reminded his readers that what he was commanding was standard policy in the other churches ("as in all the churches of the saints"; cf. 1:2; 4:17; 7:17; 11:16; 14:36). This tells us again that the Corinthian church had some serious underlying problems. Confusion and disorder in church services are not in keeping with the character of God, and such conditions dishonor Him.

In a video presented by Todd Bentley's ministry[59], we see his wife, Jessa, lose control of herself. She is swept into a "mindless frenzy." I have seen other women with the same type of spirit come to the point of almost complete exhaustion and breathlessness after such an episode. That is *not* what occurred with God's actual prophets of old. There is no example of that in Scripture.

In fact, we can look at the many examples of prophets in the Old Testament to observe their behavior and communication. Did the Old Testament prophets lose control of themselves? Does the Bible ever describe them as going into some sort of frenzy while they communicated God's truth? No. Yet this is the norm within Charismatic and NAR circles and it is *also* the norm within pagan cults like Transcendental Meditation, Yoga, and Hinduism. Make no mistake, it is demonic. It is not of God.

---

[58] http://www.soniclight.com/constable/notes/pdf/1corinthians.pdf (12/05/2017)
[59] https://www.youtube.com/watch?v=XjMYqDHbYtg (12/05/2017)

Both Todd and Jessa believe that is how God speaks to and through her. The Bentleys need our prayers because both are operating under a very serious spirit of deception.

In the same YouTube video, Jessa starts speaking around the 00:45 second mark, relating a dream involving Oral Roberts and elephants. If you don't feel like watching the entire video (and I don't blame you), jump ahead in the video to 02:58. After she says the phrase, "*...the hope from God*," her head whips to the side. It continues more violently and you can hear her hissing as well. The hissing happens numerous times while she is in her trance-like state.

What would the apostle Paul say about this? According to what he wrote to the Corinthians, he would certainly denounce it. The prophet of God was *always* self-controlled. How many times did Paul and other writers talk about the need for Christians to be in control of their faculties?

Yet we watch Mrs. Bentley and see that not only has she lost control of herself but that it clearly takes her by surprise. She also very clearly gives in and allows it to happen.

There are so many things wrong with the Charismatic/NAR movements. They resemble the Corinthian church prior to Paul's correction and discipline. The Corinthians, however, *did* seem to straighten out.

But what about today's Charismatic/NAR? Will *they* straighten out? It is seriously doubtful because too many people today want to be entertained. They want to see and experience the ethereal and supernatural. These displays of the supernatural never bring about a closer walk with God. People do not become more humble and obedient to the law of Christ. They end up simply feeding their egos.

After chasing signs and wonders, people become more focused on *SELF* and its demands. Self can never be satiated. When we give into it, it simply demands more attention. The Bible clearly and repeatedly tells us that we are to deny self and all of its yearnings. We are to take up our cross daily and follow Jesus. He lived a life of self-deprecation. He avoided catering to self. He lived to fulfill the will of God the Father and we are to do the same thing.

I hope and pray that there will be a mass exodus out of NAR and everything it represents. We need far less "gospel-tainment." What we do need, is more Christians committed to following the Lord regardless of the cost and regardless of the "experience."

CHAPTER 12 The "One Man Heresy" – The Unifying Theme Behind NAR

There is a belief that is promoted within NAR that ties everything together. It is in this belief that the most egregious and all-consuming error within NAR can be observed. This error is not solely found within NAR, however. It is often believed by those not even associated with NAR which, as *Church Watch* states, features a very "*unhealthy fascination and fixation towards Jews and the Jewish Roots movement.*"[60]

Looking back on my own life, at one time I believed that the more Christians knew and identified with Judaism, the more we would understand Christianity. While in seminary, I took both Greek and Hebrew. I did not master either subject, but studying the languages gave me greater insight into the origins of Judaism and therefore, Christianity.

I reasoned that since Jesus was born a Jew, a greater understanding of Judaism would help me in my pursuit of Him as a Christian. In reality, it is difficult to comprehend many portions of the Bible without at least a cursory knowledge of Judaism.

Seeking to understand the culture into which Jesus was born and lived is fine in and of itself. Knowing more about the feasts, the festivals, and the culture goes a long way in unlocking many portions of Scripture. The difficulty, though, is that without realizing it, a Gentile Christian can easily become entangled by the rituals of Judaism, rituals which have been fully fulfilled and replaced in Christ. This ought to be avoided.

It is easy to slide into a dependence on the Jewish rituals given to Israel under Moses. I know Christians who speak of the "Sabbath" and bemoan the idea that Christians worship on Sundays, instead of starting worship on Friday evening, the Jewish Sabbath.

There is a movement that pushes Christians to adopt the *Noahide*, which emphasizes the Seven Universal Laws of Man as listed by the Talmud[61] This is also known as the *Hebrew Roots Movement* and its emphasis on the Law ultimately replaces Jesus. It causes people to focus on *rules* and *regulations* instead of God in Christ. We know that Christians are

---

60 https://churchwatchcentral.com/2018/02/12/the-one-new-man-heresy-the-driving-theology-behind-narpostolic-unity-mainstreaming-of-hrm/ (02/13/2018)

61 Sanh. 56a

saved by *grace* alone, through *faith* alone, in *Christ* alone. We are not saved by keeping the law.

Does this also mean that Christians are exempt from having to obey the Law? Not at all. We must always seek to obey God's moral code and in Christ, we have the ability to do so. However, Christians are *not* under an obligation to obey the *ceremonial* or *religious* laws found within Judaism. I think Paul repeatedly makes this very clear throughout his God-inspired writings in the New Testament. Paul constantly stood against "Judaizers" who desperately tried to redirect Gentile Christians (as well as Jewish Christians) back to the Law. Paul regularly reprimanded them and was often brutally attacked because of it.

This push toward Judaism is occurring with the NAR movement as well. One source points out that within NAR, there is a great deal of "semantics" being played in an attempt to differentiate between words and meanings. For instance, they state the following:

"*When perusing the documents of Latter Rain theology, they constantly play semantics between 'former rain' and 'latter rain' to justify their pet theological musings. Nevertheless, there is a general theological undertone that:*

- *the Former Rain was the former covenant and covenantal blessing that Ancient Israel embraced before Christ; while*
- *the Latter Rain was the latter covenant and covenantal blessing that came with Christ.*
- *...the Former Rain was Pentecost in Acts to birth a supernatural church while*
- *the Latter Rain was to be a second Pentecost to birth a greater supernaturally-powered church before the end of the age.*"

Even though there is virtually no difference in "former" and "latter" rain, the leaders in NAR have attempted to make it so in order to push a theology that uplifts and supports a Jewish interpretation, making it applicable to Christians today. This includes observances of the following feasts:

- The Feast of Passover
- The Feast of Pentecost
- The Feast of Tabernacles

NAR leaders believe that these feasts are important for today's Christians to observe and celebrate. It is certainly permissible to *study* these feasts to see how God introduced them and ultimately connected them to Jesus. However, to begin to *observe* them as part of our fellowship with God is to revert *backward* to the Judaism that existed under Moses. The apostle Paul would say that those who do this are deliberately placing themselves under the dictates and confines of the Mosaic Law. If that is the case, then Paul also argues that the person doing that is mandated to obey *every* aspect of the Law.

NAR leaders are taking people down a very dangerous road that actually moves people *away* from Jesus. This is a common theme within many cults and why it is also believed that NAR is nothing more than a cult itself.

"*In NOLR theology, they are progressing towards the third and final age where 'the Latter house shall be greater than the former' (Sonmore, pg 12). This is why the Charismatic Movement was birthed and why we are seeing the NAR trying to militantly take over churches and establish this greater 'New Order' and 'New Wine Skin' church.*"[62]

When NAR is seriously studied, it is fascinating how similar it is to Mormonism in many ways. At the same time, it goes beyond Mormon teaching. Mormonism teaches that people can eventually become gods (just as the New Age teaches as well). NAR goes beyond this.

"*Mormonism believes one can become a god when God exalts them in obedience (Doctrines & Covenants 132:20–23). The Latter Rain take this doctrine of obedience further by claiming men can be 'gods' in this life before death. There are two forms of deification in two unique NOLR doctrines in this end-times church. Individuals are to be 'deified' and the church corporately is to be 'deified' ...*"[63]

When I was involved in the Charismatic Movement, I recall Harold Hill writing books on being a "King's kid." His most well-known book at the time was entitled, *How to Live Like a King's Kid.* The trouble with this concept is that it teaches Christians that God is essentially our "genie" and delights to give us whatever our hearts desire. Beyond this, it is fully erroneous teaching because it elevates people to being a type of deity in and of themselves.

The "King's Kids" concept imposes the idea that the Christian is a "little god" or "I AM." If our Father in heaven is "I AM," then in Christ, we share

---

[62] https://churchwatchcentral.com/2018/02/12/the-one-new-man-heresy-the-driving-theology-behind-narpostolic-unity-mainstreaming-of-hrm/ (02/13/2018)

[63] Ibid

in that divine nature, according to Peter in II Peter 1:4, but not in the same way that NAR understands it. We do not become "little gods" or any god at all through salvation and our association with Jesus. We *share* in the divine nature only so far as it aids us in overcoming sin and growing the character of Jesus within us.

As far as NAR is concerned, the "King's Kid" motif has morphed into two forms: 1) the Manifest Sons of God (MSoG), and 2) the Man-Child Company (MCC). Of course, within NAR, it is not merely relegated to those two names. To further confuse the situation, NAR has given it many names according to *Church Watch*.

- Joshua Generation
- New One Man
- New Breed
- First Fruits Company
- Overcomer Sons
- Joseph Company

Today, all of this is meant by NAR to "restore" to the Church what they believe is the lost order of the apostles and prophets. What is the reason for this? It is so the Church can powerfully unite to *bring* God's Kingdom to earth. Do not fail to miss the important implication of this last statement.

Many Christians lean heavily on the ecstatic, ethereal, and eclectic patterns of "miraculous occurrences" today. This leads Christians to pursue things that should not be pursued.

I recently talked with an individual who told me the following in an email:

"*I have had over 55 fulfilled God dreams for my life and those around me and they began at the age of 8. I did not begin to write out my prophetic dreams until 2015 because a teacher in the 5th grade told me to stop day dreaming.*

"*Both a Sheriff in 2015 told me to write down those dreams and my psychologist in 2017 told me to write down my dreams. In my life by dreams, I have seen 3 suicides which became reality later on in life.*

"*Jesus came to me twice in dreams so far. In 2007 He said this to me: You are my beloved bride who I love. May my shalom that passes all understanding cover your body, soul, spirit, and mind for all of eternity. In 2011, I read about peace in our lives when we accept Jesus into our lives."*

Tragically, I believe this person is completely deceived. I asked him why he thought Jesus needed to come to him and tell him what the Bible already teaches? Why would God need to use dreams, visions, and prophecies when He deliberately took nearly 2,000 years and forty human authors to write His completed Word?

The people who believe God still "speaks," (whether by dreams, visions, audibly, through others, or by some other means) are actually saying that God is still *writing* His Word today. If God was actually speaking to people in dreams and other ways, would what was being stated there be as authoritative as His written Word to us? Of course, it would be. Yet the trouble is that there is so much that is diametrically opposed to God's written Word. Few seem to notice, and those who do are shouted down with "don't judge!" comments.

If we look within NAR, there is a great deal that is being done and said in God's Name. It is simply passed onto people in the congregation. No one bothers to ask what the source is. No one offers any real concern for what is being said in God's Name. No one compares anything with Scripture. It is all simply accepted.

The leaders in NAR remind me of people who are actors in an improvisational skit. The first rule of that theatrical genre is always to say "*yes.*" If another actor pretends to hand you something, your job is to take it, use it, and effectively go with it, or to extend its use. Refusing to take the imaginary object handed to you shuts down the entire creative process.

In improvisation, saying "yes" to everything keeps the skit moving. Not only that, but it actively engages the other actors, allowing them to add their own interpretation to the mix knowing they won't be rejected or rebuffed.

This appears to be what's going on within NAR and the entire Charismatic Movement. It is as if a bunch of actors is all saying "yes" to each other. Watch some of the old interviews with people like Bennie Hinn on TBN with Paul and Jan Crouch. What you'll see and hear is that no matter how outlandish the stories are that are being told, everybody *agrees* with each other, and essentially encourages the other to keep going.

For example, Bennie Hinn would relate a story about how he allegedly raised someone from the dead. Paul and Jan would look wide-eyed and "marvel" giving "praise" to God for that miracle. The smiles on everyone's faces would get wider and wider. Then, Paul would "prophesy" that the Lord was going to start raising more people from the dead and he'd throw in some Scripture for good measure.

The audience would start to applaud. The smiles grow wider. Hinn might turn to the camera and speak directly to the viewers about how wonderful TBN is and how humble, and useful to God the Crouches are to the Body of Christ. It becomes a grand show of self-aggrandizement all in the Name of God.

This is NAR. People see the leaders we've talked about and all of the purported "miracles" surrounding their ministries and the average person wants to be *just like them.* They want that "power" flowing through them. They want to be able to lead others into that way of life. It is rare that they desire to lead others into a relationship with Jesus. They want the *power* that they think comes from being associated with Christ.

One website that I find interesting uses a diagram highlighting what they refer to as the Tabernacle/Man Child progression of NAR theology. NAR believes that the "outer court" of the tabernacle represents the time when a person hears the Gospel and comes to faith in Christ, through His redemptive work. This is also equated with the Feast of Passover and is simply the Salvation Stage.

The next stage is likened to the Holy Place, where only those Christians who are baptized with the Holy Spirit are allowed to go. This is equated to the Feast of Pentecost and known as the Anointed Stage.

The final stage is the Most Holy Place, which is evidenced by a person becoming a "Man Child" of God. This is allegedly when true direct knowledge of God in Christ occurs and is equated to the Feast of Tabernacles. It is when a person reaches this final stage that they become part of God's "army" that will be able to work against the evil that is occurring throughout the world. This in turn prepares the world for the coming of Jesus.

From my involvement in the Charismatic Movement, this was taught as the *first* step. After that, a *second* step was needed, which was the Baptism of the Holy Spirit. This would come over a person in a similar fashion to what occurred in Acts 2. After the second step, a person would then speak in tongues as evidence that the Holy Spirit had indeed baptized him or her with greater blessing. More steps follow.

Because of this theologically incorrect teaching, many people believe that without the baptism of the Holy Spirit (the "second blessing") they will be "second-class" Christians. Without this baptism, they will forever remain "regular" Christians, but not *empowered* Christians.

I did not remain in the Charismatic Movement long enough to learn about the Man Child stage. It has also been referred to as the "Manifest Sons of Destiny" or "Joel's Army" in the past. Names frequently change within NAR as they always attempt to remain ahead of their critics. *Church Watch* also notes that the phrase "Man Child Company" may have been renamed to "The One New Man."

...the heretical concept that the body of Christ is to become a literally 'deified' body of Jesus Christ on the earth has been renamed the 'One New Man.'[64]

There are numerous leaders within NAR who hold to this teaching. One leader, Michael Brown, has done his fair share to push this aberrant theology far and wide.

"*Michael Brown has his roots in the New Order of the Latter Rain cult...However, he, along with Jack Hayford, and other Jewish writers had their works compiled in a book titled 'Awakening the One New Man'.*"[65]

Often, these leaders play fast and loose with Scripture, either misquoting it entirely or placing a meaning on it that actually has nothing to do with *God's* intent. Sadly, people who are more intent on discovering God through ecstatic experiences do not understand how to divide His Word to discern truth rightly.

Regarding the One New Man theology, Jack Hayford states, "*The quest for **One New Man**-for acknowledging, pursuing, and embracing this spiritually **essential precursor** of **God's "last days spiritual awakening and awaiting worldwide revival**" (see Rom. 11:12, 15, 25) **-must become an essential,** vital **to us, in us and through us all.** It is critical because the Word of God exhorts us to pursue it. But today it is also at a crisis point of **needed awakening** in the living Church; remembering the times call for it-both past times as well as today's unfolding times.*"[66] (emphasis in original) This statement may appear confusing to readers, but what Hayford is essentially stating is that Christian need to pursue the "one man status,"because through it, we will awaken spiritually to God's coming worldwide revival. It is (allegedly) what will bind all to God and bring God back to the earth in victory.

What Christians need to understand is that God does not ask us to do any sort of work to enable His return. Those times have already been set

---

64 https://churchwatchcentral.com/2018/02/12/the-one-new-man-heresy-the-driving-theology-behind-narpostolic-unity-mainstreaming-of-hrm/ (02/13/2018)

65 Ibid

66 https://churchwatchcentral.com/2018/02/12/the-one-new-man-heresy-the-driving-theology-behind-narpostolic-unity-mainstreaming-of-hrm/ (02/13/2018)

by God. Moreover, Jesus will return of His own volition, His own strength, and His own determination according to the times and seasons set by the Father. There is *nothing* that Christians can do to hasten this event.

NAR, and other groups connected to it or influenced by it, would have us believe that the second coming of Jesus is dependent upon the Church. They teach that as God pours out His Spirit throughout the world, He is enabling Christians to draw closer to Him for a spiritual empowering. Complete with signs and wonders, this "empowering," will ultimately overcome evil and "allow" Jesus' return to this earth.

What these people do not realize is that their anti-biblical beliefs actually denigrate the power and sovereignty of the Almighty God. It is a tremendous disservice to God to make Him appear dependent on people.

During the Triumphal Entry into Jerusalem, (just days before Jesus was betrayed, arrested, illegally tried, convicted, and given a death sentence) people were busy shouting out praises to Him as He rode on the back of a donkey. The religious leaders were aghast and told Jesus to tell the people to stop shouting "Hosanna." Do you recall what Jesus' response to them was at that time?

He answered, "I tell you, if these were silent, the very stones would cry out." (Luke 19:40 ESV)

Imagine that. Jesus is saying that if He told the people to stop doing what they were doing, the very rocks would cry out. Nature would pick up and do what the people were rightly doing because God in the flesh was in their presence!

Even if no one in the world performed God's purposes, He would *still* accomplish His will for this world! It will be done whether people do what they are called to do or not.

NAR and other groups emphasize the miraculous. They chase after signs and wonders, believing that they are somehow more spiritually mature than the average Christian who does the Father's will without supernatural experience.

Because of this inordinate emphasis on the sign gifts, the very calling of Christ to fulfill the Great Commission often gets sidelined. Yet, those within NAR would say that they *are* fulfilling the Great Commission as evidenced by those who "come" to Jesus. The unfortunate part is that those who "come" to Jesus, rarely come to Him as Savior.

Simply attend one of these conferences or watch one of the online videos to observe the "signs and gifts" raining down on people, granting them "repentance." This is diabolical because they are *not* receiving salvation at all. They are simply being affected by some supernatural display that, in many cases, has little or no connection with Scripture. People splay out on the floor. They laugh until they can't laugh anymore. They twirl and dance around, falling flat on their backs. They uncontrollably shake all over, jerking their heads from side-to-side without restraint.

This is akin to what occurs within the New Age movement during the opening of the Pineal Gland or Third Eye. Currently completely off-limits to Christians, NAR operatives are working feverishly to bring this technique into the mainstream church, and they appear to be succeeding. Christians need to be aware of this epidemic problem and reject it fully.

The goal of NAR is to bring all people together under the apostate belief that God is creating His children into "little gods." As followers grow in that awareness, God will do greater things through them than were done through Jesus. Corporately, they will then bring Jesus to the earth in His Second Coming.

The only person that will come to center stage because of NAR and the New Age Movement is the coming *Antichrist.* I guarantee you that if the Antichrist came on the scene now, leaders within NAR would welcome him with open arms and would likely bow down to worship him! People within the New Age Movement would do the same thing, which should tell us that there is something terribly wrong with that picture.

My goal is to alert people to the reality of error that is preached and promulgated with the NAR movement. There is nothing good within NAR. It thrives on ecstatic experiences believed to be from God, but that originate from godless sources.

Satan needs all the power he can obtain. When the Antichrist first comes to earth, he will appear to be the "Savior" humanity has long been searching for. It won't be long, however, before his true identity will reveal itself. Revelation 6-18 makes this indelibly clear.

The Antichrist will ride onto the scene as a "Savior," capturing more and more power until his authority is utmost. He will then try to dispose all the world's armies to accomplish the one thing he has determined to do – keep Jesus from returning to this earth! He will try to keep our Holy God from returning to the earth that He created!

I say this with utmost concern. NAR is the "Christian" version of the New Age Movement. They both seek the same thing, whether they know it or not. They both look to bring that individual to this earth whom they believe to be the Christ. According to Revelation 6, the person to show up on the scene as the first seal is opened is the "Rider on the White Horse."

This person comes to conquer politically. His appearance on a white horse will cause many to assume that he is the actual Christ, the true Savior. He won't be. The Bible makes this so clear.

For your sake and the Lord's sake, please steer clear of any group that emphasizes signs and wonders. Even the Pentecostals disavow NAR; so should you.

If signs and wonders are not used by God today, then what is the alternative to drawing close to God, to learning His will, and to living that will in our lives? Read on. In the next chapter, we will outline what I believe is the biblical way to discern God's will for your life. It is not a way that is littered with the ecstatic. It is, however, a very profound way of understanding God and His will for your life.

CHAPTER 13 The Biblical Way

In searching for God, proponents of Dominionism, NAR, Kingdom Now, and even New Age, believe there is a shortcut to finding God's will. This shortcut manifests itself in the ethereal and the ecstatic, the signs and wonders. These, they say, are evidence that God is moving and working and are automatically taken as proof of God's Presence. Discernment is normally absent.

We're moving now into another series that defines the biblical way of drawing closer to God. This approach takes longer and is seemingly far more pedestrian in style, but unlike the Signs and Wonders Movement, it actually produces character in the Christian's life.

This particular path is not for the person who seeks instant gratification. It is for the Christian who is willing to travel down the proper road to develop the relationship that salvation enters us into – with the God of the universe.

Have you ever placed a "fleece" before God? Have you ever opened the Bible and placed your finger on a verse determining that the action and the verse will speak to a specific need in your life and provide direction from God? Have you ever used Promise Boxes? Have you ever just been frustrated over the question of attempting to discern God's will for your life?

Here are some of the terms we often use in regard to God's will. Do any of these words or phrases ring true with you as you have sought to learn God's will for your life?

- discover
- learn
- seek
- find
- uncover
- divine
- gain understanding
- direct
- lead

- comprehend
- seek after

You may have other words or phrases that you can add to that list, but certainly, the point is clear. In many ways, Christians do everything they know to do to discover God's will for their lives. It makes sense to do this because it shows true dedication to God's purposes and we are taught that God has a unique will for each of His children.

We want to live His will. In fact, we endeavor to be like Jesus in that regard. Jesus clearly, on a daily, and even moment-by-moment basis, lived in the exact center of God the Father's will for His life. Not once did Jesus ever fail to complete the Father's will for Him. Christ's life is a model for us to follow and the committed Christian, knowing that he will never perform God's will perfectly in this life, understands that this daily attempt should be made.

So then, why is it when we discuss God's will, the terms we use always seem to imply that He doesn't really want us to know it? We speak of "finding" or "discovering" God's will as though God wants to keep it a secret, or that He's intent on making it difficult for us to "uncover"?

The truth is, in an attempt to know God's will, most of us have probably placed "fleeces" before the Lord and done a number of other things in the hopes of unlocking the combination. It is a common thread among Christians.

Dr. Bruce Waltke has taught Old Testament and Hebrew at Dallas Theological Seminary, Regent College, Westminster Theological Seminary, and several other institutions of higher learning. He has published numerous books and articles. One book, in particular, is the subject of this series, entitled, *Finding the Will of God.* Waltke's premise is that Christians have been doing things wrong in a big way. The reason we've been doing things wrong is because we fail to understand the difference between how saints in the Old Testament understood God's will and how those in the New Testament and beyond understand it.

Waltke believes it starts with the vocabulary we use when we discuss God's will. We often use terms or phrases that make it sound as though God is very reluctant to reveal His will to us, yet without doubt, He expects us to walk in His will with every step we take.

Waltke asks an important question in his introduction. "*Why would a God who wants us to do His will hide it from us? Why do Christians go through such convoluted, painful efforts to know it? His will needn't be hidden or elusive; a mystery, a puzzle, an enigma. The answer we seek already lies in our theology – what we believe…The concept is very simple – don't you think we will be better able to understand His will when we are more like Him?*"[67]

In essence, Waltke believes that what we think about God (which should stem from His Word, our theological base) will translate how we determine God's will for our lives. If we think incorrectly about God and knowing God, then we will likely not be correct in determining His will for our lives. It all starts with our theology. While this does not mean we have to become professional theologians overnight, all Christians need to have a basic (and growing) understanding of who God is, how He works, and how He has chosen to communicate with us. If we do not have this basic understanding, we will be mercilessly tossed to and fro on an endless sea of waves.

Waltke spends the introduction answering the following three questions regarding our theology.

- Why is it true?
- Why is it essential?
- Why should it be my way of life?[68]

Waltke states that theology is truth. He means, of course, the correct understanding of theology, as God has revealed it in His Word, not what we might *think* it means. It is a careful distinction and one that we must pay careful attention to so that we can ultimately "rightly divide" or correctly handle, God's Word.

He also states that correct theology is an essential part of spiritual formation. Waltke does not mean "spiritual formation" in the sense that it is used today in the emergent church. For Waltke, it means our growth in Christ. He connects our theology with our growth, just as it is described throughout Scripture, especially by the New Testament writers.

It is very easy to forget that God's Word is living. It is active. It is not simply a collection of stories on a few thousand pages. It is God's revelation to us about Himself and His plans for this world. Because God is alive, living, and powerful, so is His Word. How we understand God's Word has a direct impact on us, our lives, and our spiritual growth in Christ. If we have erroneous theology (as exists within much of the signs and wonders arena), our lives will be negatively impacted, and not only will we cease to

[67] Finding the Will of God, by Dr. Bruce Waltke, 1995, p. 7
[68] Finding the Will of God, by Dr. Bruce Waltke, 1995, p. 17

grow more like Christ, but we will do great spiritual harm to ourselves and possibly others.

In response to the three questions he posed, Waltke states that theology is a way of life. In other words, what we believe should translate to how we live. Let's stop to consider the fact that in its early days, Christianity was called "the way." Why it was called that?

We know that Jesus referred to Himself as "the way, the truth, and the life..." *(John 14:6).* Jesus also spoke of every person traveling down a road that leads to eternity. People traveling that road without Christ will continue traveling until they reach their final eternal destination, which is hell. Comparatively few will move off that path onto what Jesus calls the "straight and narrow," which leads to another eternal destination, heaven. The point is that we are all moving toward an end goal.

It is actually the same with Christianity. Once we get on that straight and narrow path, we continue to move along that path and our goal and desire is to move according to the Lord's will for our life.

If we are committed to the "way" of Jesus Christ, (a way that compels the transformation of lives and cultures into a conformity with the ultimate realities of God) our theology (what we believe about God), will shape our lives (how we live for God). As we are led by the Spirit into a fuller understanding of Him, we experience what Scripture calls "the will of God." [69]

As a Christian, would you say you are committed to submitting yourself to God's will on a daily basis? It is almost certain that this is your desire. Apart from simply being thoroughly compliant and simply letting things happen to you as they will, how do we learn what God's will is for us?

What is interesting about Waltke's book are the various sections. He first discusses *How Pagans Divine the Will of God*, followed by *God's Will in the Old Testament.* This is all under the section, *Part One: God's Will: a Pagan Notion.* His next part, *Part Two: God's Program of Guidance* explains over several chapters exactly how God seeks to guide Christians.

Waltke discusses how the Israelites determined God's will in the Old Testament and helps us understand why that no longer applies. He also delves into the ways pagans determined their god's "will," normally by

---

[69] Finding the Will of God, by Dr. Bruce Waltke, 1995, p. 19

various forms of divination, an act thoroughly forbidden for Israel and Christians.

As we open up this series with future articles, we will provide insights into *God's Program of Guidance.* Waltke covers this topic in six sections and incredibly, it is likely simpler than the ways we have attempted to discern God's will for us in the past.

If you're like me, there is something we may have been missing where God's will is concerned. I can recall times of great frustration and even confusion. Many times, I've said something like, "Wouldn't it be nice if an angelic messenger arrived at my front door each morning with an envelope detailing God's will for my life?"

That would be nice, or so we'd like to think. If that happened, however, we would miss the important lesson that God has built into the process of discerning His will. That lesson is character development. God wants us to develop Christ's character as we walk with Him and come to understand His will for us. This is one of the big reasons He forbids Christians from the many forms of divination. They all circumvent character development. There are other reasons for the prohibition as well, but failure to develop character is certainly an important aspect of it.

CHAPTER 14: What Every Christian Needs to Know

We've been discussing aspects of the Signs and Wonders Movement in previous posts. The emphasis there is on manifestations believed to be from God. It would seem instead that these manifestations are demonic activity and self-delusion. Anytime self is elevated, it will take advantage of a situation.

Yet those within the Signs and Wonders Movement will tell you they are led by God daily, that they know and understand what His will is for them, and that He works His will in and through them as evidenced by those signs and wonders. This is their perspective and they believe it should be so for all Christians.

However, as introduced in our most recent article, Christians need to rethink the way they contemplate and seek God's will. We noted that theology – what a person believes about God – informs that person's thinking and decisions related to His will. Unfortunately, all too often, Christians seem not to know what the Bible teaches regarding God's will or how to biblically discern it. As a result, these same Christians (and we've all been there) will fall back on superstitious ways of trying to divine His will.

The bottom line is that if we fail to read, study, and memorize His Word, we will be operating under our own energy and wisdom, which amounts to nothing. We will tend to create situations that will likely fall under the category of "wood, hay, and stubble" when we stand before our Lord at the BEMA Seat of Judgment *(I Corinthians 3:12-13).*

We also mentioned how often Christians use the wrong verbiage regarding God's will. We often speak of "finding" or "discovering" God's will as though He wants to keep it secret from us. This idea is not found in Scripture. If not, then why do so many Christians seem to believe that God is stingy in revealing that will? We wind up turning ourselves into pretzels at times doing whatever we can to come up with the right combination of words or actions that will ultimately release knowledge of God's will to us.

There are no instances of seeking or finding God's will after Acts 1:24, in which the disciples drew lots to select Matthias as a replacement for Judas. There are dreams, visions, and revelations after this, but never in the context of seeking God's will. It is not divination, seeking to probe the divine mind, but rather it is revelation given by God to His people. After

Pentecost there is no instance of the church seeking God's will through any of the forms of divination. There is a much better way, a far more biblical way; a way that, with continued practice and commitment, will allow us to learn God's will in the fashion that He intends.

...God's method of revealing His mind with regard to specific choices in a perplexing situation before Pentecost are not normative for the church. Apart from the lot in Acts 1, the church lacks both prescriptive and perceptual warrant in the New Testament.[70]

From this point, Waltke moves on to discuss what he believes is the truly biblical way in which all Christians should walk in God's will. Waltke believes that God Himself has provided a "...six-point program of supervised care in directing His elect." Waltke also believes the order in which we follow these six steps is extremely important.

It should come as no surprise that his first point is that Christians must read the Bible daily. We should read it, study it, meditate on it, and memorize it. Doing all of this will bring us closer to God since His Word is "*...living and active, sharper than any two-edged sword, piercing to the division of soul and of spirit, of joints and of marrow, and discerning the thoughts and intentions of the heart*" *(Hebrews 4:12 ESV).*

It stands to reason that if God's Word is all that Hebrews claims it is, then it will impact our lives and draw us closer to the Living God. Let's not forget Paul's words to Timothy in II Timothy 3:14-17, where the apostle proclaims among other things that the Bible "*is God-breathed and useful for teaching, rebuking, correcting and training in righteousness, so that the man of God may be thoroughly equipped for every good work.*"

What this means is patently obvious. As we read and study God's Word, it has the power to teach, rebuke, correct, and train us in the way of righteousness. That way of righteousness means living God's will in and through our lives. If we fail to read His Word daily, it cannot do any of these things. The result is that we will constantly be relying on the way we feel about God, about our lives, and about how we think God might be directing us.

What is also very interesting about the Bible (reading it and studying it), is that it provides knowledge about many aspects of God's will for our lives. Waltke brings this out frequently. He cites I Thessalonians 5:15-18 where Paul outlines some very basic instructions for how every Christian should live. According to Paul, we should always seek after the good, we should always pray and rejoice, we should not repay evil with evil, and we

---

[70] Dr. Bruce Waltke, Finding the Will of God, p. 70, 71, 72

should be thankful in all situations. These things are God's will for every person. No Christian is exempt from them.

But how is this done? When someone wrongs you, the natural (fleshly) tendency is to want to avenge that wrong. We want to repay their evil with some evil of our own. Is this how Jesus responded? Never. If we call ourselves followers of Jesus, we must take the ramifications of His words and actions seriously enough to want to see them duplicated in our life.

When faced with the temptation to repay evil with evil, what is the biblical response? During that time of temptation to react with evil, the Holy Spirit can remind us of the truth of I Thessalonians 5:15-18, and we can pray Scripture back to God asking Him to help us overcome that temptation. Two things will happen. First, the fact that we are speaking Scripture will act as a rebuke to the forces behind the temptation, including our flesh, which has been crucified with Christ. Second, repeating the Scripture will also allow the Holy Spirit to bring it alive within us so that we do not give in to the temptation to return evil for evil.

But what if you don't have any verses hidden in your heart? You are left with only prayer and your hope that God will be able to help you without the tremendous weapon of the Scriptures.

Can you imagine going into battle without a weapon or without a helmet to protect your head? Can you imagine having portions of your body uncovered? No soldier goes into battle without body armor for protection, along with the proper weapons to take out the enemy. God has given us both in His Word. Paul writes about it, clarifying his meaning to us:

Put on the whole armor of God, that you may be able to stand against the schemes of the devil.

Stand therefore, having fastened on the belt of truth, and having put on the breastplate of righteousness, and, as shoes for your feet, having put on the readiness given by the gospel of peace. In all circumstances take up the shield of faith, with which you can extinguish all the flaming darts of the evil one; and take the helmet of salvation, and the sword of the Spirit, which is the word of God, praying at all times in the Spirit, with all prayer and supplication. (Ephesians 6:11, 14-18 ESV)

It is vital to take every available piece of armor into battle, and every day we wake in this life, we enter the battle. Satan works to thwart God's plans and purposes for us, and he will do whatever he is allowed to ensure our defeat. Christians too often make this very easy by not reading the very

Word of God that is alive, active, and able to discern the thoughts and intention of the heart.

If you're not already doing this, start reading His Word daily. Study and memorize it so that the Holy Spirit can use it when you face temptations that will come to you. This is what Jesus did. His demonstration of Scriptural knowledge in the face of temptation was an example of how we must prepare daily for spiritual warfare. Read His Word. Study it. Memorize it. Meditate on it. Know God through it.

CHAPTER 15 Living God's Will

It is important for readers to understand that I am not an expert in living out God's will. None of us is. It is important to realize that it is an ongoing process as part of our sanctification. I'm not writing about this subject because I perfectly live out God's will in my life. I'm writing this as much to me as to you. If you benefit from it, all the better, but I benefit from writing it out because it helps to cement it into my own life.

Previously, in discussing Dr. Bruce Waltke's book, *Finding the Will of God*, I noted that he provides a history of how pagans (and too often, Christians) use numerous forms of what can only be called "divination" to determine God's will. From there, Waltke moves into a discussion of how the Christian should learn and live God's will. Far from what those within the Signs and Wonders Movement advocate, determining God's will is made easier (and far less mystical, ecstatic, and controversial) when we are living lives that move us closer to God.

Waltke introduces a six-point program that every Christian should put into place if they take seriously the goal of living out God's will. He also emphasizes that the order in which those six points are followed by the Christian makes a great deal of difference.

He begins with the one thing (aside from actual salvation) that every Christian needs to immerse himself in: reading, studying, and memorizing God's Word. Without this, there is no real theological base. He indicates that our theology defines what we believe about God, in that, if our theology is wrong, or non-existent, then we cannot rightly expect to progress in our faith. As a result, we will not be able to discern God's will in life's varying circumstances.

In God's Word, we learn the structure of God's will that applies to every Christian without reservation. There are things that everyone needs to be doing. In each of Paul's letters to the churches, he provides general instruction. By general, I'm referring to how every Christian should live. Here's an example of what I mean.

For this is the will of God, your sanctification: that you abstain from sexual immorality; that each one of you know how to control his own body in holiness and honor, not in the passion of lust like the Gentiles who do not know God. (I Thessalonians 4:3-5 ESV)

In the above text, notice that Paul precedes the command with the words, "For this is the will of God." What is the will of God? It is what he says next, that all Christians should abstain from sexual immorality, that we should all control our bodies, and that we should not be driven by passionate lusts. These are commands of an apostle and he tells us that obedience to these things is the will of God!

This brings up a couple of questions. First, how does a person do this when the temptations can be so strong? Second, how does obeying these aspects of God's will help us determine God's will in other situations that are far more specific to us?

There are only two ways we can obey Paul's commands here. One, we can either attempt to obey them in our own strength and energy, or two, we can rely on God's strength to overcome the temptation when it raises its head. I think most would agree that obeying in our own strength may get the job done. We may have successfully ignored the temptation. Is this what Jesus did?

In Matthew 4, Jesus went head-to-head with Satan and He didn't use His own strength. He quoted Scripture and allowed the power of God's Word to defeat the enemy. It was in this way that Jesus overcame every temptation He faced throughout His life, not just during that time in Matthew 4.

When faced with the type of temptation Paul speaks of in the above passage, what is the best defense for it? God's Word! If we commit those few verses (or others like them) to memory, then the Holy Spirit can bring them to our minds during times of temptation. As we then repeat those verses to ourselves, the power and living nature of God's Word will defeat the temptation without us having to use our energy to do so. In using our own energy, we are doing what we can to squelch the temptation. Certainly, that's better than nothing, but the truth is that God wants to work in and through us and He does that best when we've hidden His Word in our hearts. This is exactly what Jesus did.

Let's use another example, also from I Thessalonians 5:15-18.

See that no one repays anyone evil for evil, but always seek to do good to one another and to everyone. Rejoice always, pray without ceasing, give thanks in all circumstances; for this is the will of God in Christ Jesus for you.

Look at that list from Paul. He says we should avoid doing evil to someone when they do evil to us. We should always seek the best for everyone. Beyond this, we should always be thankful, rejoicing all the time. We should pray without ceasing – which means we should always be talking with God – and be thankful in all circumstances. Why? Because all these things are God's will for us. It is God's will that we should be like Jesus. Paul provides us with an example of how Jesus lived.

When reviled, Jesus did not insult in return. When He was slapped in the face, He didn't turn around and slap the person who slapped Him. The Gospels tell us just how much Jesus prayed. He was always thankful, and even as He hung dying on the cross, He was able to ask the Father to forgive those directly responsible for His death. They were not aware that they were executing an innocent Man, who was and remains God.

Do you live in the way Paul describes above? I don't. I'm learning. Based on an individual's personality and the way he responds, he may face the temptation to react in kind more than others might. It varies from person to person, but every Christian must strive to be obedient to God so that we please Him. God can then recreate the character of Jesus in us through these trying situations. It is God's will that every Christian live like this. Regarding this, there can be no disagreement.

How does living like Jesus help us learn, discover, and discern God's will in specific situations in our lives? What if someone wants to determine which college to go to, which job to accept, which person to date, which person to marry, or where to live?

Being obedient to God in the small things – the things that Jesus, Paul, and others teach us in God's Word – will recreate our character. This is unlike the Signs and Wonders Movement, where character development is largely absent. In fact, what we often see is the exact opposite of Christian maturity. The theology of groups like this is usually aberrant and because of it their character is less than stellar. This is certainly not what God wants to recreate in them.

As we develop a lifelong willingness to be obedient to God in the things He has revealed in His Word, we become more mature in Him. This happens as Christ's character is recreated within us. As we become more mature, we are in a better position to test all things to know God's will. However, if we do not read His Word, if we do not study it or memorize it, we are bypassing God's route for us to know His will.

We must read His Word, but we must also learn to properly interpret Scripture as well. How often we Christians take things completely out of context and believe we speak truth!

How many times have you been chastened by some well-meaning Christian who hears you critiquing what a Christian leader has taught, with the words, "Don't judge"? They have no idea the context of that command.

They simply assume that Christians are not to go around negatively critiquing anything or anyone, especially a known Christian leader. However, Christ was speaking of the tendency of Christians to judge the heart condition of someone or the motivations behind their actions. These are things we cannot see and so we should ensure that we are not guilty of judging someone's motives or heart. Acts 17 proves that Christians should absolutely critique what others teach. Paul approved the practice and so did Jesus *(Matthew 7:1-5)*.

When I was in Bible college, I was taught that the Bible should be allowed to interpret itself. This is the best way to learn what God is telling us. Why is this true? Because God wrote the entire Bible through some 40 human authors over a period of 1,600 to 2,000 years. Because God is responsible for every word and sentence, we can be assured that what He wrote in Genesis corresponds in some way to what He wrote in Matthew or Revelation. The Bible connects with itself. For a person to understand theology it is necessary to understand that the Bible is both cohesive and comprehensive.

Admittedly, it takes years to come to a point of understanding the flow and pattern of the Bible just like it takes years to master a musical instrument. Yet the beginnings of understanding can come soon if the Christian is willing to apply himself to the study of God's Word.

Waltke uses numerous examples in his book where he believes Christians misinterpret Scripture. One common mistake is taking verses out of context. He believes this is the case with the regular misunderstanding of Proverbs 3:5-6 and James 1:5. Look them up and ask yourself what you think they mean.

Waltke's repeated point is that the Christian does not "*divine God's will. One lives God's will as one comes to know Him through His Word.*"[71] However, this only comes to individuals who are committed to obeying God.

God clearly wants Christians to be loving, especially to one another. How often is the exact opposite of this on display to the world? God wants us to refrain from all forms of sexual immorality. God wants us to no longer lie, cheat, steal, or commit other crimes. If we are not faithful in obeying these things, why would God be willing to live other aspects of His will through us? It won't happen.

---

[71] Dr. Bruce Waltke, Finding the Will of God, p. 86

CHAPTER 16 Focusing on God or Satan?

I've mentioned that at one point in my life I was involved in the Charismatic Movement. I've also noted that I eventually left that movement. However, later on, because I did not realize the connection to the Charismatic Movement, I spent a bit of time attending a "deliverance ministry" church. Thankfully, my involvement was short-lived.

That so-called deliverance ministry was similar to many others like it. People there believed that it was important for Christians to take a direct stand against the powers of darkness wherever they were found. If a Christian was "demonized" or oppressed, spiritual people should come forward, lay hands on them, and cast out the demons. This also applies to the belief that demons take control of certain areas in the world geographically. Often, Daniel 10 is the go-to section of Scripture that is used to prove this. The concept doesn't appear to exist in the New Testament.

Unfortunately, as I found out, many in the Deliverance Ministry Movement appear to be making things up as they go. The Bible itself is relatively silent on such a ministry. Yes, there were times when Jesus went head-to-head with Satan, rebuking him and telling him to leave Him. That does not constitute exorcising Satan from a specific realm. There is really nothing in Scripture that allows us to build a solid case for having a deliverance ministry. However, there are many people and groups who consider such ministry necessary.

Let's consider some biblical facts. First, while demonic activity is real, the only thing that gets through to the Christian is what God allows. Christians already have the victory against the powers of darkness because of the work of Christ in defeating the power of sin. This is clear in God's Word.

Second, deliverance ministries seem unaware of the approach Jesus Himself used in Matthew 4. When Jesus faced temptation from Satan, He met that temptation with Scripture. He did not use His own strength. He did not debate with Satan. He did not do what those in deliverance ministry often do. Jesus fought temptation with Scriptures. He had spent His growing up years reading, studying, and memorizing the Scriptures. That should also be our model.

Third, while there are certainly instances of demonic activity in Scripture, there also appears to be an absence in the Bible of anyone going directly against these warriors of Satan, with a few noticeable exceptions.

For instance, we know that an unfallen angel who came to Daniel was kept at bay for three weeks by the Prince of Persia in the spiritual realm *(Daniel 10)*. However, Daniel was unaware of this. Daniel did not enter the fray even after he was informed of the problem. It was beyond his purview. It was Michael the Archangel who provided assistance to the first angel.

Fourth, though Jesus Himself spoke directly to Satan, when Paul speaks of turning a man over to Satan, he is speaking of putting him out of the protective environment of the local church *(1 Corinthians, 1 Timothy)*. Paul did not directly take on Satan.

Fifth, even though Jesus and some of His disciples cast out demons, there is no instruction on how or even if we are to do that. In fact, Jesus seems to downplay the issue. When His disciples return giddy about the fact that even demons listened to and obeyed them, Jesus cautioned them that what was more important was the fact that their names were written in the Book of Life *(Luke 10:20)*. Salvation is the ultimate act of deliverance.

As a whole, the problem with the Deliverance Movement is its focus. It seems to be a very subtle redirecting of the Christians' focus from God to Satan. It concerns me.

If anyone could have taken on Satan directly and removed him from geographical areas, it would be Jesus, and that's not going to happen until He returns. Why hasn't He "bound" Satan now? Because it is yet future.

Our victory in Christ is already complete, and we've addressed that in several articles recently. We already have everything we need for our spiritual growth, our maturity, and our victory in Christ because the Holy Spirit lives within us and seals us. Though this is true, Paul tells us that we need to "put on" God's armor to fight the good fight *(Ephesians 6)*. These are not material weapons, but metaphorical concepts that represent realities in verses 10 through 18. Righteousness is ours in Christ. The shield of faith is our belief in God and His ability to save. The Sword of the Spirit is God's Word, which we must read, study, and hide in our heart. It takes some effort on the part of the Christian to become a good soldier for Christ.

Paul says our battle is not against flesh and blood but against spirits in the heavenly realms. He is not saying we need to take them on directly. He's saying that when someone wrongs us or tempts us, we need to realize that they are likely motivated by the unseen evil forces. Because of that, we should not react to them in kind but in gentleness and love, as Jesus did. We also have what we need to overcome any temptation that comes our way.

I've read numerous articles on the internet that provide a great deal of alleged insight into the dark forces of the spiritual realm. This information typically comes from extra-biblical sources.

I've also noticed that there are even lists of the types of demons by name. Paul tells us that demons are lying spirits, but I don't see where demons have specific names that allow them to attack believers by using specific sins *(II Corinthians 11:14-15)*. "Legion" was one such group of demons, but it represented many demons inhabiting one man *(Mark 5:9)*. Jesus asked their name, and that was the response. It went on biblical record that their individual names do not matter.

Jesus said that Satan was a murderer from the beginning and the Father of Lies *(John 8:44)*. Satan's demons simply do the same thing Satan does – they work to thwart God and attack believers. They seek to destroy using weaknesses inherent in each Christian to overcome that Christian. James explains this clearly in James 1:14-15. *"But each person is tempted when he is lured and enticed by his own desire. Then desire when it has conceived gives birth to sin, and sin when it is fully grown brings forth death."* The sinful desires are already resident within us because of our fallen natures.

Dangle a piece of cooked liver in front of me, and I'm not the least bit interested. Dangle a New York Strip steak, and you've got my attention. Maybe gluttony is a problem for one Christian. Lust is a problem for another. Anger is an issue for yet another Christian. Satan's angels can easily figure out which buttons to push based on our weaknesses as they observe us. They simply use the weaknesses they see to their advantage, hoping to make us crash and burn.

Again, our victory comes first by reading and studying God's Word. Secondly, it comes through prayer and constant communication with God. Thirdly, it comes through memorizing Scripture and hiding it in our hearts so that the Holy Spirit can recall it during times of temptation. Do you want victory? Do these things. It may be easier to yell at spiritual entities who may or may not be there. But how does that develop godly character?

Many Christians will tell you that they suffer from problems and maladies and often attribute these to demonic activity. People within deliverance ministries support this notion. However, Christians who appear to be suffering from certain maladies may actually have a physiological problem that needs to be diagnosed by a medical professional.

However, on one occasion, Jesus healed a man and later told him, *"See, you are well! Sin no more, that nothing worse may happen to you" (John 5:14 ESV)*. The implication is that the man's lifestyle caused his sin. Jesus was saying, avoid the sin, and you'll remain whole.

To attribute everything to Satan is a bit shortsighted. Sometimes, it's simply health-related. I submitted DNA samples for genetic testing several years ago. I learned that there are certain substances that my body cannot tolerate so I now avoid them like the plague.

For instance, I have the MTHFR genetic issue, which means, among other things, my body cannot tolerate or process folic acid. Yet our bodies need folic acid, so what do I do? I now ensure that my folic acid is in its methylated form, FOLATE, which is digestible by my body. I also ensure that I eat green, leafy vegetables as well. It surprised me to learn how many food products on store shelves are "enriched" with folic acid, so I must avoid them for my health.

Symptoms of folic acid "overdose" include extreme fatigue, tiredness, and may even cause what outwardly appears to be forms of depression. Someone from a deliverance ministry would likely have told me that I was "demonized." No, I was simply ingesting things my body rejected, leaving me with unpleasant side-effects.

I now fully believe that many of the symptoms that people (including Christians) suffer from are often due to food and drink. Longtime readers of my blog will recall the articles I've written about my journey to health, which started about five years ago. My health has greatly improved because I now avoid anything with folic acid, high fructose corn syrup, gluten, corn, and several other things. I try to buy non-GMO and gluten-free as often as possible. My wife and I eat very simply now, but I continue to see other Christians with a range of problems that I believe can be traced back to what they consume.

This is not to minimize satanic attacks on Christians. They are real. Paul experienced it as well in II Corinthians 12. Notice that he did not direct his apostolic authority at the "messenger of Satan" who inflicted him with some problem. Instead, verse 8 tells us that he went to the Lord three times. If deliverance ministry is legitimate, why didn't Paul simply take on that satanic messenger directly in his apostolic authority, banishing it to the outer realms or the pit? Jesus did not send demons to the pit either *(Mark 5)*.

The best way to face temptations is with the Sword of the Lord, God's Word. Our focus is to be on God, not ourselves, and certainly not on Satan. As God allows, demons will attack Christians wherever they are weakest. What are your weaknesses? Demons will attempt to cause a Christian to become angry, to lust, to want to murder someone, etc., because of the weakness that is inherent within that particular Christian due to our sin nature. It is not because a particular demon specializes in one particular sin and goes by that name.

Regardless of the tendency toward sin in each Christian, the path to victory is the same for us all. It is to hide God's Word in our hearts. When we face temptation, we can recall Scriptures that speak to that area and the power of God's Word will cause Satan and his minions to flee, just as Satan fled in Matthew 4.

This emphasis on deliverance ministry is unbiblical. The greatest deliverance a person can ever have is to be delivered from Satan's Kingdom of Darkness to God's glorious Kingdom of Light. That happens when a person receives salvation. That is true deliverance.

CHAPTER 17 Context Means a Great Deal

We have transitioned from highlighting the history of what has become the modern Signs and Wonders Movement, most noticeably, the New Apostolic Reformation (NAR) Movement. Since the very early 1900s, nearly each decade has had a distinctly named movement, but each is tied to and based on signs and wonders. Moreover, these various movements became prominent due to philosophers embracing the concept of existentialism. Existentialism basically elevates feeling and emotion over reason and becomes the final authority for determining truth.

I reviewed a set of articles which all tied together under the banner of knowing God's will. People within the Signs and Wonders Movement determine God's will through manifestations that they firmly believe are from God in their midst. I believe that I've shown this is not only not the best way, but it often provides erroneous information because of the heavy reliance on the nature of a person's feelings.

It is interesting how often Christians tend to take things out of context. It happens to all of us. It is, unfortunately, very much a part of the Signs and Wonders Movement. The many "prophetic words" routinely given by leaders within this movement are often either a jumble of out-of-context Scripture or exceedingly generalized "prophecies" about some new move of God.

This happens, whether in NAR or in our own personal lives, due to one main issue. We fail to take into consideration the context of the Scripture. This has been the case with Rabbi Jonathan Cahn's numerous books where he tries to build a case for some future event that he implies the Lord revealed to him. These cases are built on one or two verses from Scripture. He then attempts to take these few verses and apply them generously to the United States. His overall attempt to link America with Israel is clearly seen throughout his books, yet the Scripture has no such link. The verses he uses often solely apply to the nation of Israel, but he tries desperately to prove a link between Israel and America. Therefore, he concludes that what happened to Israel could also happen to America unless there is revival.

Of course, aside from the nation of Israel, God is not interested in saving nations. This is not a popular notion today because so many Christians in America believe God will save our land if we pray and dedicate ourselves to helping Him do just that. This inevitably leads to a belief in some form of Dominionism (the belief that Christians must engage the culture to revive America as a theocratic nation). As more of the world's nations are converted to God, then ultimately, Jesus will be able to return to this planet. Dominionism denies the true sovereignty of God by its very nature and definition. Dominionism, sadly, is the result of not only taking verses of Scripture out of context but of seeing other verses allegorically, instead of literally.

A good example is when you might hear someone from the Word of Faith (WOF) or Prosperity Gospel Movement proclaim that Joshua 1:8 proves that God wants us to "prosper" or, in their vernacular, become wealthy.

This Book of the Law shall not depart from your mouth, but you shall meditate on it day and night, so that you may be careful to do according to all that is written in it. For then you will make your way prosperous, and then you will have good success. (Joshua 1:8 ESV)

Taking this verse out of its natural context, it's not difficult to see how it can be twisted to mean something it does not mean. The idea here is that meditating on God's Word will pave the way to success and prosperity. This is hardly what Joshua meant when he spoke those words. The context fleshes out the full meaning.

The first chapter of Joshua opens with God's commissioning of Joshua to lead the Israelites into the Promised Land. Recall that Moses was prohibited from doing so because of his sin in Numbers 20. Moses struck the rock so that water would pour forth instead of simply speaking to that rock. The rock represented Christ and this incident occurred years before when Moses was told by God to strike the rock *(Exodus 17)*.

In Numbers 20, Moses was told to simply speak to the rock. Both incidents represented the first and second coming of Jesus. He came first as the Suffering Servant and was abused, beaten, and crucified. Because Moses struck the rock on the second occasion, he ruined the motif God wanted to present about Jesus' second coming, where He will come in power and victory. No one will abuse Him then. As another result, God prohibited Moses from leading the Israelites into the Promised Land.

Appointed by God, Joshua took over the task of leading the people into the Promised Land. Joshua stood up to point out to the Israelites that if they dedicated themselves to God, if they meditated on His Word if they hid His Words in their heart, and if they worked to observe all that was written in the Law, then they would be prosperous and would have good success. What is this referring to here?

The Israelites knew that going into the Promised Land, God would use them as His arm of judgment against the many pagan nations that lived there. It is in that sense that Israel would be "prosperous" and would have "good success." Of course, it was intended that Israel would be the example to all other nations of how to live for God. They failed miserably time and time again in this.

God was not promising to make the Israelites wealthy. He was promising to be with them, to guide them, to gain the victory over the pagan nations through them. But Israel had to do something for that to happen. Israel had to immerse itself in God's Word. They had to be willing to study, memorize, and hide God's Word in their hearts so that they could observe it in daily living.

In other words, Joshua was telling the people that only if they were willing to adopt God's ways from the heart would they be "prosperous" and have "good success" in vanquishing God's foes from the land. There was still a great deal of work ahead of the Israelites and a great deal of responsibility rested on their shoulders before God. If they did their part of the bargain, there would be success. If not, there would be failure.

Joshua was essentially telling them that if they spent time memorizing and meditating on God's words, it would become part of them. They would then live outwardly what was inside them. God would work in and through them to bring His goals and purposes to fruition. It is the same for the Christian, except that we are not here to take land. We are here to free prisoners from Satan's kingdom *(Matthew 28)*. That is the scope of our commission.

Joshua 1:8 says absolutely nothing about either Jews or Christians becoming wealthy if they will simply meditate on God's Word. Yet, there have been some who like to use this verse out of context to persuade people that God exists so that His followers will become rich and live their earthly lives out in prosperity. This is not what the Bible teaches. If it is, Jesus and His apostles missed that point entirely!

If we are going to see God's will unfold in our lives, then we need to be reading, studying, and memorizing His Word as our starting place. We must be willing to put these habits into practice for God to enable us through the power of His Word. Beyond this, we must be extremely careful to not take things out of context, which allows an erroneous and often dangerous meaning to be applied to His Word.

God wants us to prosper, but to prosper in our spirits. While He certainly may bless some people financially, He does so only for His purposes. Too many false preachers today teach that God wants you rich, and that if you're not rich, you're doing something wrong. They say that as you "plant" seeds of faith in large sums of money (often to their ministries), that God will bless you. Surprisingly, the only ones who are getting rich are the false teachers. There is one church in the Atlanta area where you cannot become a member unless you are willing to let the finance committee of that church see record of your bank account, how much you make, and where you spend your money. This gives them the advantage of determining whether a person gives at least 10% to the ministry. If that person doesn't, it means they are not qualified to be a member. This is diametrically opposed to what is taught in the New Testament regarding giving.

To know God's will means knowing and thoroughly understanding His Word. It cannot be emphasized enough that we must be careful in guarding ourselves against taking Scripture out of context. The damage that is done is great. We must always consider the full meaning of a verse or verses of Scripture when we choose passages to memorize. This is only accomplished when we consider the verses surrounding the verse or verses we choose to memorize.

This is the danger in trying to find God's will by simply opening the Bible and pointing randomly to a verse of Scripture as some do. God does not guide us through that method of divination.

If you want to know God and His will, start with reading, studying, meditating, and memorizing His Word. Of course, the very first step is in becoming a Christian. God reveals His will to those who are dedicated to Him, who seek Him first, who dedicate their lives to being true bondservants. A bondservant is a slave who wants to be a slave. They are also referred to as "indentured servants," those who willingly attach themselves to another as lifelong servants.

God is looking for people like this, those who are willing to deny themselves so that God can use them as an open vessel through which He can work. Is that you? Are you willing to submit yourself to Him as Jesus did?

So if there is any encouragement in Christ, any comfort from love, any participation in the Spirit, any affection and sympathy, complete my joy by being of the same mind, having the same love, being in full accord and of one mind. Do nothing from selfish ambition or conceit, but in humility count others more significant than yourselves. 4 Let each of you look not only to his own interests, but also to the interests of others. Have this mind among yourselves, which is yours in Christ Jesus, who, though he was in the form of God, did not count equality with God a thing to be grasped, but emptied himself, by taking the form of a servant, being born in the likeness of men. And being found in human form, he humbled himself by becoming obedient to the point of death, even death on a cross. (Philippians 2:1-8 ESV)

Jesus emptied Himself, not of His deity, but of His self-will, in order to allow God the Father to work in and through Him 24 hours a day, 365 days a year for the duration of His earthly life. It is what allowed Him to offer Himself as a propitiation for sin – yours and mine.

If we are going to follow Jesus, how can we do any less? For the record, I do not do this perfectly. But like you, I am learning how to submit myself to Him so that He can work in and through me to accomplish His will. The more I submit to Him, setting aside my own desire to satisfy myself, the more He shows me His will.

CHAPTER 18 The Long Road

In the end, being a Christian requires time, patience, growth, and a constant desire to do the things that God wants us to do to bring Him glory. There are no shortcuts. There is no instant gratification.

The organization referred to as NAR today has an extensive history of deceiving people throughout Christendom. It has pulled people off the path and away from God despite its claims to the contrary.

For the truly committed Christian, following God takes time, just as physically growing takes time. Maturity in Christ does not happen overnight, nor does it happen as the result of ecstatic experiences.

Brother and sisters, may you draw close to Him daily through His written Word. It is an amazing gift that He has provided for us. He wants us to know Him. He wants us to seek Him. He wants us to understand what He has revealed to us about Himself.

If you are not reading His Word every day, may I encourage you to do so. Your reward will be great.

CHAPTER 19 The End?

Do you know *when* you will die? Are you aware of the *day* and *hour* when you will slip from this life into eternity? I'm betting you are not privy to that information. So why are you living as if you *do know when it will happen?* Putting a decision about Jesus off until another day is taking a huge chance because of the fact that you do not know when you will die. That is plainly simple, and logic alone demands that you do not put this decision off. Yet you do, because the thought of becoming a Christian makes you feel uncomfortable.

You wrongly believe that to become a Christian means that you have to change in a major way *before* Jesus will accept you. It means to you giving up the things you love now because if you love them, then obviously they are wrong, and God does not love them.

You are putting the cart before the horse. You must understand that God is not rejecting you. He is not standing there, tapping His foot, demanding that you eliminate those things that He does not like before you can come to Him for salvation.

If you (or anyone) could do that, you would not *need* His salvation at all. It is because you and I do things that are not pleasing to Him that we need His salvation.

What do you do that you would like to do no longer? Do you drink excessively until you cannot control it? Do you play around with drugs? Do you eat too much food until you have become overweight, lethargic and sickly?

What other things are in your life that you do not like? Are you drawn to illicit extra-marital affairs? Do you have a problem with lust? Are you a shopaholic? Do you tend to tell lies a great deal because it makes you feel important, or to hide things about your life?

Do you find that you do not like people and you would prefer to be around animals or out in the woods than around people? Are you a workaholic? Do you place a high value on money and you find that you work very hard to obtain it?

Here's the problem. The enemy of our souls comes to us and tells us that God will never accept us until we get rid of those things. He lies to us that God essentially wants us "perfect" before He will be willing to meet us and grant us eternal life. This is completely untrue.

The other lie that our enemy tells us is that we should not become a Christian because the fun in our life will fly out the door. We will no longer be able to drink or do the fun things we enjoy now. We start to think that coming to God means becoming a doormat for people and having to fill our life with things we do not want ever to do.

These are all lies, and unfortunately, too many people believe them. First of all, God does not expect you to be "perfect" before you come to Him for salvation. If that were the case, no one would be able ever to approach Him.

Secondly, God does not say that He is going to take away all the things we enjoy and replace them with things we hate. What is wrong with enjoying the lake on your boat? What is wrong with spending a day with the family fishing or just relaxing in the mountains? There is nothing wrong with these things.

What God *will* do is begin to remove the things that have ensnared you so that life is actually draining from you, but you are not aware of it. For instance, maybe you drink excessively, and you have tried everything you can think of to quit. You have gone to AA meetings, spent thousands of dollars on this program or that, and you have even used your own will power to free yourself from the addiction to alcohol, all to no avail.

The question is not: *do I need to quit before I come to Jesus?* The question is: *am I willing to allow Him to work in and through me to take away the addiction I have to alcohol?* Do you see the difference? Are you willing to allow Him to work in you to break that addiction so that you will become a healthier person, one who is able to think straight and one who learns to rely on Him for strength? That is all He wants you to be able to do. He knows you cannot break that addiction (or any addiction for that matter) with your own strength and willpower. Are you willing to allow Him to do it in and through you?

What if you are a workaholic? What if you have "things" like a boat, a house in Cancun, a large bank account, four cars, and more? Do you think that God is going to ask you to give it up, or worse, do you think that God will simply come in and take all of that from you? I know of nothing in Scripture that tells us He will do that.

What God will do with all of those who come to Him trusting Him for salvation is one thing, which begins the moment we receive salvation and will continue until the day we stand before Him. He will begin to create within us the character of Jesus (cf. Ephesians 2:10).

Here is a verse from the Old Testament that was said originally through the prophet Ezekiel to the people of Israel. While this was specifically stated to the Jews, it is applicable to all who receive salvation through Jesus Christ.

"*I will give you a new heart and put a new spirit within you; I will take the heart of stone out of your flesh and give you a heart of flesh. I will put My Spirit within you and cause you to walk in My statutes, and you will keep My judgments and do them*" (Ezekiel 36:26-27).

God is speaking here through Ezekiel, and He is saying that He will give the people a new heart of flesh, removing that old heart of stone. This is God's responsibility. God is the One who makes that happen. We are told in the book of Hebrews that God is the Author and Finisher of our faith (cf. Hebrews 12:2). This tells me that God is the One who changes me from within so that over time, my desires are slowly turned into His desires.

I recall years ago thinking that God wanted to do everything in my life that I did not want Him to do. I fell into the asinine belief that He wanted to change everything about me. What I learned is that yes, there are things that God does want to change about me. However, there is a lot that God originally gave me that He has also enhanced and used for His glory.

Maybe you are a workaholic who thinks that working hard is something God does not want you to do. This is not necessarily the case. He may have given you the ability and the knowledge to work in the area of finance for a great purpose. All He may wind up doing is dialing back your workaholic tendencies so that you have more time to enjoy your family and study His Word.

But you say you smoke, or drink, or use illegal drugs, and you don't want to give those up. As I stated, you can't give those up under your own power, and the fact that you have tried so many times has proven it to you.

But God knows what is and what is not good for you. Are you willing to *allow* Him to work in you to change your desires so that you no longer want to smoke, use illegal drugs, or drink nearly as much?

Then you say that you believe God wants to make you a Christian, so you can become miserable. Isn't that what most Christians are – miserable? Not the Christians I know, and certainly not me, my wife, or our children.

Where does the Bible say that God wants us miserable? You will not find it. What God wants is for us to be blessed, and that begins when we receive salvation from His hand.

You know, if we would stop and take the time to consider the fact that this life is exceedingly short if we compare it to eternity, we will then realize that there is nothing so important that it should keep us from receiving Jesus as Savior and Lord.

Unfortunately, too many people do not consider the brevity of life. They think they will live forever, or at the very least, they will die when they are really old and gray. That will come too soon. Even though I have just recently turned 54, it still truly seems like yesterday that I was a young boy fishing in the Delaware River near Hobart, New York. There I spent many Saturdays fishing and simply enjoying being outdoors. How did life go by so very quickly? How could that have happened?

It has happened, and I am at a point in life where not only do I realize that this life is short, but I actually look forward to spending eternity with Jesus after this life. Does that sound morbid to you? It shouldn't, because by comparing this life to eternity, we should get a sense of what is truly important.

God does not expect us to become Mother Theresas. He does not necessarily expect us to give up everything and become missionaries in outer Mongolia. What God expects is for us to simply allow Him to change our character as He sees fit.

Over time, we may well find that we have simply stopped swearing without realizing it. Our desire for cigarettes or alcohol has nearly evaporated. Illicit affairs no longer enter the picture.

We also may find that some of the things we want to eliminate in our life become more pronounced. Often the enemy will do this to cause us to focus on something that God is not even doing in our lives at that point. It causes tension, frustration, and self-anger.

If you have gotten to this point in your life and you have not dealt with the question about Jesus, it is about time you do so. You need to stop what you are doing and realize a couple of things before you go through another minute in this life.

- **Sinner**: you need to realize that you are a sinner. You have sinned and you will continue to sin. Sin is breaking the laws that God has set up. We all sin. We have all broken God's laws and that breaks any connection we might have had with God. Sin pushes us away from Him.

  Romans 3:23 says, "*For all have sinned, and come short of the glory of God.*" That means you and that means me. All means all.

That is the first step. We need to recognize and agree with God that yes, we are sinners. I'm a sinner. You are a sinner. This results in God's anger, what the Bible terms "wrath."

- **God's Wrath**: Romans 1:18 says, "*For the wrath of God is revealed from heaven against all ungodliness and unrighteousness of men, who suppress the truth in unrighteousness.*"
- This is as much a fact as the truth that we are all sinners. Because we are sinners – by breaking God's law(s) – God has every right to be angry with us and ultimately destroy that which is sinful. If we choose to remain "in" our sinful states throughout this life, we will – unfortunately – be destroyed with the rest of sin.
- Fortunately, there *is* a remedy, and it is salvation.
- **God's Gift**: In the sixteenth chapter of Acts, a jailer asks Paul this famous question: *what must I do to be saved?* The question was asked because Paul and Barnabas had been imprisoned, and while there, they began singing praises to God.
- God then sent a powerful earthquake that opened the doors to all the prison cells, yet no one escaped. When the jailer arrived, he saw that everyone was still in their cells, and after seeing that miracle (what prisoner would not want to escape from prison?), turned and asked what he must do to be saved. He was speaking of the spiritual aspect of things. He wanted to know how he could be guaranteed eternal life.
- The answer Paul gave the man was, "*Believe on the Lord Jesus Christ, and thou shalt be saved, and thy house*" (Acts 16:31).
- This is not head knowledge or intellectual assent. This is *believing from the heart*. In fact, Paul makes a very similar statement in another book he wrote, Romans. He says, "*That if thou shalt confess with thy mouth the Lord Jesus, and shalt believe in thine heart that God hath raised him from the dead, thou shalt be saved. For with the heart man believeth unto righteousness; and with the mouth confession is made unto salvation*" (Romans 10:9-10).
- When we fully believe something, we confess that it is true. It must begin in the heart because that is where the will is located. We must want to believe. We must endeavor to believe. We must seek to believe.
- We must stop giving ourselves all the reasons to deny or ignore Jesus. As God, He became a Man, born of a virgin. He clothed

Himself with humanity that He might show us how to live, and in so doing, would keep every portion of the law.

- If Jesus was capable of keeping every portion of the law, then He would be found worthy to become a sacrifice for our sin – yours and mine. If He became a sacrifice for our sin, then all that we must do is embrace Him and His sacrificial death.

In short then, to become saved we must:

1. Admit (we sin)
2. Repent (want to turn away from it)
3. Believe (that Jesus is the answer)
4. Embrace (the truth about Jesus)

We **admit** that we are sinner, that we have sinned. This is nothing more than agreeing with God that we have broken His law. Can you honestly say that you have not broken God's law? If you admit to breaking even the "smallest" law, then you are a lawbreaker.

After we admit that we have sinned, the next step is found in **repenting**. Some believe that repenting is actually moving away from sin. This author believes that it is a willingness to move away from sin, and there is a difference.

As we have already discussed, it is impossible to stop sinning. Human beings simply cannot do it because as long as we live, we will have a sin nature, which is something within us that gives us a propensity to sin. As long as we have this inner propensity to sin or break God's laws, we will never be perfect in this life.

We cannot one day say, "Lord, I promise to stop sinning." If we do that, we are only kidding ourselves and setting ourselves up for major failure. We cannot stop sinning in this life. The most we can do is *want* to stop sinning and then spend the rest of our lives allowing God to create the character of Jesus within us, slowly, little by little.

Repenting is to decide that you no longer want to do the things that keep us out of heaven. We no longer wish to break God's laws. It is not promising God that we will never sin again.

Once we admit, then repent, we must **believe**. This is one of the most difficult things to do because believing that Jesus died in our place, that He lived a perfectly sinless life, is extremely difficult to believe. Our minds cannot grasp that truth. We must ask God to open our eyes to that truth so that we can embrace it.

While on the cross next to Jesus, the one thief joined the other thief in ridiculing Jesus. Then, all of a sudden – as we read in Luke 23 – this same thief that had just been ridiculing Him now turned to Him with a new understanding.

It was this new understanding that prompted the thief to say to Jesus, "*Lord, remember me when you come into your Kingdom.*" Jesus looked at the man and responded to him, "*Today, you will be with me in paradise.*"

What had occurred in the mind and heart of that thief from one moment to the next? One thing, and that one thing was that God opened the thief's eyes so that he could see the truth. It was as if the blinders fell off and he now saw and understood who Jesus was, even to the most cursory degree that Jesus was dying not for Himself, but for others.

It was this understanding, this awareness, which prompted the man to ask Jesus to simply be remembered. Jesus went way beyond it to promise the man that he would be with Jesus that day in paradise.

Please notice in Luke 23 that there is nothing in the chapter that tells us that the man promised Jesus he would give up sin, or that he would never sin again. There is nothing that tells us that thief took the time to enter into a final deathbed confession of his sins so that he could be absolved.

The thief made no promises to Jesus at all. What he experienced was the truth of who Jesus was and what Jesus accomplished for humanity. Jesus accomplished what we cannot. What is left is for each person to *admit*, *repent*, *believe*, and *embrace*.

Let me clarify here that though we do not see any verbal repentance from the thief, we know that he did repent. He admitted as well. How can we know this? It is simply due to the thief's complete about-face with respect to his attitude toward Jesus. One minute, he was ridiculing Jesus, and the next, embracing Him. This is important. There is no way he could have or would have *embraced* Jesus had he not been humbled by the truth *about* Jesus.

Once the thief saw the truth, he was instantly humbled. Within himself, he knew that he was a sinner, and in fact the text states that this is what he told the other thief dying next to him. "*But the other answering rebuked him, saying, Dost not thou fear God, seeing thou art in the same condemnation? And we indeed justly; for we receive the due reward of our deeds: but this man hath done nothing amiss*" (Luke 23:40-41). Something happened within the heart of the one thief. In one moment, the thief went from harassing Jesus to recognizing his own sinfulness and then ultimately asking for grace, which was freely given to him.

Whether he said it or not, the thief went from haughtiness to humility in a very short space of time, and it was all because he saw the truth about Jesus. That truth helped him realize that he deserved his death and what would happen to him after death. He understood that Jesus did not deserve death.

From here, the thief fully embraced the truth about Jesus and was rewarded with eternal life because of it. He did not come off the cross to be water baptized. He did not list a long litany of offenses against God. He recognized the truth about Jesus, was humbled, and embraced that truth!

This is what each of us needs to do. We cannot give in to the lie that tells us that we are not good enough, or we have not given up enough before God will accept us. We must reject the lie that says we must somehow earn our salvation.

Jesus has done everything that is necessary to make salvation available to us. The only thing that is left for us is to see the truth. Once we see that truth, it should humble us to the point of embracing Jesus and all that He stands for and is to us.

The eighth chapter of Romans begins with the fact that all who trust Jesus for salvation are no longer condemned...*ever*. All of my sins – past, present, and future – have not only been forgiven, but canceled. It is because of my faith in the atonement (death) of Jesus that God is able to cancel all of my sins, even the ones that I have not committed yet. This does not make me eager to commit them. It makes me want to do what I can to avoid sinning.

If you do not know Jesus, please do not put down this book without deliberately *believing* that He is God, that He died for you by the shedding of His blood on the cross, and that He rose three days later because death could not keep Him. Do you believe that? If you do not yet believe it, do you *want* to believe it? If so, then simply ask God to help you come to believe all that Jesus is and all that He has accomplished for you. God will answer your prayers and you may either receive instantaneous awareness of all that Jesus is and has done, or it may be a *growing* awareness over time. In either case, it is the most important decision you will ever make.

Turn to Him now and pray for knowledge of the truth and an ability to embrace it. Please. He is waiting for you.

Ask Yourself:

1. Do you *know* Jesus? Are you in *relationship* with Him? Have you had a spiritual transaction according to John 3?
2. Do you *want* to receive eternal life through the only salvation that is available?
3. Do you believe that Jesus is God the Son, who was born of a virgin, lived a sinless life, died a bloody and gruesome death to pay for your sin, was buried, and rose again on the third day? Do you *believe* this?
4. Do you *want* to *embrace* the truth from #3?
5. Pray that God will open your eyes and provide you with the faith to begin believing the truth about Jesus. Ask Him to help your faith embrace the truth, realizing that you are not good enough to save yourself and that your sin will keep you out of God's Kingdom without His salvation.
6. Pray as if your life depended upon it because *it does*!

Resources for Your Library

BOOKS:

- Basis of the Premillennial Faith, The, by Charles C. Ryrie
- Biblical Hermeneutics, by Milton S. Terry
- Daniel, the Key to Prophetic Revelation by John F. Walvoord
- Dictionary of Premillennial Theology, Mal Couch, Editor
- Daniel, by H. A. Ironside
- Daniel: The Kingdom of the Lord, by Charles Lee Feinberg
- Daniel's Prophecy of the 70 Weeks, by Alva J. McClain
- Exploring the Future, by John Phillips
- Footsteps of the Messiah, by Arnold G. Fruchtenbaum
- Future Israel (Why Christian Anti-Judaism Must Be Challenged), by E. Ray Clendenen, Ed.
- God's Plan for Israel, Steven A. Kreloff
- Israel in the Plan of God, by David Baron
- Israelology, by Arnold G. Fruchtenbaum
- Moody Handbook of Theology, The by Paul Enns
- Most High God (Daniel), by Renald E. Showers
- Mountains of Israel, The, by Norma Archbold
- Pre-Wrath Rapture Answered, The, by Lee W. Brainard
- Prophecy 20/20 by Dr. Chuck Missler
- There Really Is a Difference! by Renald Showers
- Things to Come, by J. Dwight Pentecost
- What on Earth is God Doing? By Renald Showers

WEBSITES Resources

- https://1eternitymatters.wordpress.com/
- https://churchwatchcentral.com/
- http://watch-unto-prayer.org
- http://www.thomas.littleton.bluecollarsaints.org
- http://bluecollarsaints.org
- http://www.studygrowknowblog.com
- http://planobiblechapel.org/constable-notes/
- https://christianpublishinghouse.co/2018/03/14/the-danger-from-within-the-church/
- https://christianpublishinghouse.co/2018/03/05/what-should-you-look-for-in-order-to-find-the-one-true-christian-church/

Bibliography

A., M. E., Harris, R. L., Archer Jr., G. L., & Waltke, B. K. (1999). *Theological Wordbook of the Old Testament.* Chicago: Moody Press.

Akin, D. L. (2001). *The New American Commentary: 1, 2, 3 John.* Nashville, TN: Broadman & Holman .

Akin, D. L., Nelson, D. P., & Peter R. Schemm, J. (2007). *A Theology for the Church.* Nashville: B & H Publishing.

Alden, R. L. (2001). *Job, The New American Commentary, vol. 11* . Nashville: Broadman & Holman Publishers.

Anders, M. (2005). *Holman Old Testament Commentary - Proverbs* . Nashville: B&H Publishing.

Anders, M., & Butler, T. (2002). *Holman Old Testament Commentary: Isaiah.* Nashville, TN: B&H Publishing.

Anders, M., & Lawson, S. (2004). *Holman Old Testament Commentary - Psalms: 11.* Grand Rapids: B&H Publishing.

Anders, M., & McIntosh, D. (2009). *Holman Old Testament Commentary - Deuteronomy.* Nashville: B&H Publishing.

Archer, G. L. (1982). *New International Encyclopedia of Bible Difficulties, Zondervan's Understand the Bible Reference Series.* Zondervan Publishing House: Grand Rapids, MI.

Archer, G. L. (1985). *The Expositor's Bible Commentary, Vol. 7: Daniel and the Minor Prophets.* Grand Rapids: Zondervan.

Archer, G. L. (2007). *A Survey of Old Testament Introduction. Revised and expanded ed.* Chicago: Moody.

Barker, K. L., & Bailey, W. (2001). *The New American Commentary: vol. 20, Micah, Nahum, Habakkuk, Zephaniah.* Nashville, TN: Broadman & Holman Publishers.

Bercot, D. W. (1998). *A Dictionary of Early Christian Beliefs.* Peabody: Hendrickson.

Blomberg, C. (1992). *The New American Commentary: Matthew.* Nashville, TN: Broadman & Holman Publishers.

Boice, J. M. (1986). *Foundations of the Christian Faith.* Downers Grove, IL: IVP Academic.

Borchert, G. L. (2001). *The New American Commentary: John 1-11* . Nashville, TN: Broadman & Holman Publishers.

Borchert, G. L. (2002). *The New American Commentary vol. 25B, John 12–21.* Nashville: Broadman & Holman Publishers.

Brand, C., Draper, C., & Archie, E. (2003). *Holman Illustrated Bible Dictionary: Revised, Updated and Expanded.* Nashville, TN: Holman.

Breneman, M. (1993). *The New American Commentary, vol. 10, Ezra, Nehemiah, Esther.* Nashville: Broadman & Holman Publishers.

Brooks, J. A. (1992). *The New American Commentary: Mark (Volume 23).* Nashville: Broadman & Holman Publishers.

Butler, T. C. (2005). *Holman Old Testament Commentary - Hosea, Joel, Amos, Obadiah, Jonah, Micah* . Nashville: Broadman & Holman Publishers.

Christiaan, E. (2015). *TITHING: Exposing One Of The Biggest Lies In The Church.* New York, NY: BookPatch LLC.

Cole, R. D. (2000). *THE NEW AMERICAN COMMENTARY: Volume 3b Numbers.* Nashville: Broadman & Holman Publishers.

Croteau, D. A. (2001). *Perspectives on Tithing: Four Views.* Nashville, TN: B&H Academic.

Elwell, W. A. (2001). *Evangelical Dictionary of Theology (Second Edition).* Grand Rapids: Baker Academic.

Elwell, W. A., & Beitzel, B. J. (1988). *Baker Encyclopedia of the Bible.* Grand Rapids, MI: Baker Book House.

Ferguson, E. (2003). *Backgrounds of Early Christianity.* Grand Rapid, MI: Eerdmans Publishing Co.

Ferguson, E. (2005). *Church History ,Volume One: From Christ to Pre-Reformation: The Rise and Growth of the Church in Its Cultural, Intellectual, and Political Context.* Grand Rapids, MI: Zondervan.

Garrett, D. A. (1993). *Proverbs, Ecclesiastes, Song of Songs, The New American Commentary, vol. 14.* Nashville: Broadman & Holman Publishers.

Garrett, D. A. (1993). *The New American Commentary: Vol. 14 (Proverbs, Ecclesiastes, Song of Songs).* Nashville: Broadman & Holman Publishers.

George, T. (2001). *The New American Commentary: Galatians* . Nashville, TN: Broadman & Holman Publishers.

Gonzalez, J. L. (2010). *Story of Christianity: Volume 2: The Reformation to the Present Day (The Story of Christianity).* New York, NY: HarperCollins.

Hill, E. M. (2010). *What Preachers Never Tell You About Tithes & Offerings: The End of Clergy Manipulation & Extortion.* Atlanta, GA: SunHill Publishers.

Jameson, T. (2016). *The Tithing Conspiracy: Exposing the Lies & False Teachings About Tithing and the Prosperity Gospel.* Carrollton, GA: Inspired Word Publishers.

Lea, T. D., & Griffin, H. P. (1992). *The New American Commentary, vol. 34, 1, 2 Timothy, Titus.* Nashville: Broadman & Holman Publishers.

MacArthur, J. (2005). *Fool's Gold?: Discerning Truth in an Age of Error.* Wheaton, IL: Crossway.

MacArthur, J. F. (2013). *Strange Fire: The Danger of Offending the Holy Spirit with Counterfeit Worship.* Nashville, TN: Thomas Nelson.

Martin, D. M. (2001, c1995). *The New American Commentary 33 1, 2 Thessalonians* . Nashville, TN: Broadman & Holman.

Martin, G. S. (2002). *Holman Old Testament Commentary: Numbers.* Nashville: Broadman & Holman Publishers.

Mathews, K. A. (2001). *The New American Commentary vol. 1A, Genesis 1-11:26* . Nashville: Broadman & Holman Publishers.

Matthews, K. A. (2001). *The New American Commentary Vol. 1B, Genesis 11:27-50:26.* Nashville: Broadman and Holman Publishers.

Melick, R. R. (2001). *The New American Commentary: Philippians, Colossians, Philemon, electronic ed., Logos Library System.* Nashville: Broadman & Holman Publishers.

Melick, R. R. (2001). *The New American Commentary: vol. 32, Philippians, Colissians, Philemon.* Nashville, TN : Broadman & Holman Publishers.

Morris, L. (1992). *The Gospel According to Matthew, The Pillar New Testament Commentary.* Grand Rapids, MI(; Leicester, England: W.B. Eerdmans; Inter-Varsity Press,.

Mounce, R. H. (2001, c1995). *Romans: The New American Commentary 27.* Nashville: Broadman & Holman.

Mounce, W. D. (2006). *Mounce's Complete Expository Dictionary of Old & New Testament Words.* Grand Rapids, MI: Zondervan.

Polhill, J. B. (2001). *The New American Commentary 26: Acts.* Nashville: Broadman & Holman Publishers.

Renee, R., & Harper, C. (2014). *The Tithing Hoax: Exposing the Lies, Misinterpretations & False Teachings about Tithing.* Morrisville, NC: LuLu Press.

Richardson, K. (1997). *The New American Commentary Vol. 36 James.* Nashville: Broadman & Holman Publishers.

Robertson, N. (2008). *Tithing : God's Financial Plan.* Matthews, NC: Norman Robertson Media.

Rooker, M. F. (2000). *The New American Commentary, vol. 3A, Leviticus.* Nashville: Broadman & Holman Publishers.

Ryrie, C. C. (1989). *A Survey Of Bible Doctrine.* Chicago, IL: Moody Publishers.

Ryrie, C. C. (1999). *Basic Theology.* Chicago: Moody.

Schreiner, T. R. (2003). *The New American Commentary: 1, 2 Peter, Jude.* Nashville: Broadman & Holman.

Scott Jr., J. J. (1995). *Jewish Backgrounds of the New Testament* . Grand Rapids, MI: Baker Publishing Group.

Smith, G. (2007). *The New American Commentary: Isaiah 1-39, Vol. 15a.* Nashville, TN: B & H Publishing Group.

Smith, G. (2009). *The New American Commentary: Isaiah 40-66, Vol. 15b.* Nashville, TN: B&H Publishing.

Stein, R. H. (2001, c1992). *The New American Commentary: Luke.* Nashville, TN: Broadman & Holman .

Stuart, D. K. (2006). *The New American Commentary: An Exegetical Theological Exposition of Holy Scripture EXODUS.* Nashville: Broadman & Holman.

Taylor, R. A., & Clendenen, R. E. (2007). *The New American Commentary: Haggai, Malachi, , vol. 21A* . Nashville, TN: Broadman & Holman Publishers.

Vine, W. E., Unger, M. F., & White Jr., W. (1996). *Vine's Complete Expository Dictionary of Old and New Testament Words.* Nashville, TN: T. Nelson.

Vunderink, R. W., & Bromiley, G. W. (1979–1988). *The International Standard Bible Encyclopedia, Revised (,* . Grand Rapids, MI: Wm. B. Eerdmans.

Waltke, B. (1995, 2016). *Finding the Will of God.* Grand Rapids, MI: Eerdmans.

Walvoord, J. F., & Chafer, L. S. (1974). *Major Bible Themes: 52 Vital Doctrines of the Scripture Simplified and Explained.* Grand Rapids, MI: Zondervan.

Warren, R. (2002). *The Purpose Driven Life: What on Earth Am I Here For?* Grand Rapids: Zondervan.

Wells, A. B. (2007). *Tithing: Nailed To The Cross.* Bloomington, IN: Author House.

Wood, D. R. (1996). *New Bible Dictionary (Third Edition).* Downers Grove: InterVarsity Press.

Wood, L. J., Harris, R. L., Archer Jr., G. L., & Waltke, B. K. (199). *Theological Wordbook of the Old Testament.* Chicago: Chicago: Moody Press.

Woodbridge, J., & James III, F. A. (2013). *Church History, Volume Two: From Pre-Reformation to the Present Day: The Rise and Growth of the Church in Its Cultural, Intellectual, and Political Context.* Grand Rapids, MI: Zondervan.

www.ingramcontent.com/pod-product-compliance
Lightning Source LLC
Chambersburg PA
CBHW060017050426
42448CB00012B/2796

* 9 7 8 1 9 4 5 7 5 7 9 7 6 *